KARUNANIDHI

KARUNANIDHI

A Life in Politics

SANDHYA RAVISHANKAR

HarperCollins *Publishers* India

First published in India in 2018 by
HarperCollins *Publishers*
A-75, Sector 57, Noida, Uttar Pradesh 201301, India
www.harpercollins.co.in

2 4 6 8 10 9 7 5 3 1

P-ISBN: 978-93-5277-919-2
E-ISBN: 978-93-5277-920-8

Typeset in 11.5/15.2 Apollo MT Std at
Manipal Digital Systems, Manipal

Printed and bound at
Thomson Press (India) Ltd.

The first is for the first I loved.

To the leprechaun lady with shining green lanterns for eyes,
too big nose, skin of over-ripe mangoes,
who smelt always of Yardley rose talcum powder,
and who forgave and loved unconditionally until the end.

Beloved grandmother Jaka Avva,
I know you would have been the proudest.

CONTENTS

FOREWORD

Biography exists in different epistemological spaces. From being regarded by historians as something of a stepchild and the stuff of academic whimsy, the relevance of biographical writing to an analytic understanding of our past is much better accepted today. As a form of writing, biographies are not always contained by explanations of their subject's actions in the context of the prevailing social or political environment. Insofar as they explain the motives of people in an individualistic manner, biography is a form of psychology. Finally, as narratives, biographies are, particularly when written well, a form of creative non-fiction. They allow for the freedom to the select the stories the biographer wants to relate or highlight and provide the licence for the biographer to set the tone, the pace and the pitch in the telling.

Inevitably perhaps, Sandhya Ravishankar's biography inhabits all the three spaces. Her book, which follows an unusual structure, is cleaved in two halves. The first is a largely linear account of Karunanidhi's life, beginning with his birth, tracking his political rise, and his years as Tamil Nadu's chief minister. The second half has a thematic quality, dwelling on topics such as Karunanidhi's complex relationship with his supporter-turned-political rival

MGR – subjects that the author has apparently chosen because of the interest they hold and the light they throw on Tamil Nadu's politics.

The other distinguishing feature in the structure of the book is framed around a series of incidents or events, some disparate, many interconnected. Interspersed with quotes, this is very much a journalist's work – one in which it is possible to read sections of the book as if they were separate stories about Karunanidhi's long and event-filled life. It is a reminder that while human lives are a linear continuum, the stories distilled from them are the ones we believe make up their very essence.

Mukund Padmanabhan

Editor, *The Hindu*
April 2018

PROLOGUE

We hunkered down every time a vehicle passed by. Sitting inside a car on a humid September afternoon in Chennai, even with the windows rolled down, was stifling. The clock ticked ever so slowly towards 4 p.m.

My colleague Satish Kumar and I had arrived at CIT Colony in central Chennai at 2.30 p.m. itself. We were employed with the young, energetic news channel CNN-IBN at the time – he, a video journalist, and I, a cub reporter, in my first reporting job.

The pressure had mounted by September 2007 from our headquarters in Delhi. My boss and then bureau chief had gone to London on a three-month Chevening scholarship, leaving me to handle the explosive political situation. I had no contacts, except for a few well-meaning senior journalists who did not hesitate to give me numbers. Perhaps they felt sorry for me. Dravidian politics can be daunting even for the most experienced hand. Luckily, I had the brashness of youth on my side. Worse, I was smarting from a dressing down.

The chief minister of Tamil Nadu at the time was the Dravida Munnetra Kazhagam's (DMK) M. Karunanidhi, a blessing for reporters starting their careers. Press conferences were regular and sometimes held even twice a day – at the Secretariat in the afternoon and at Anna Arivalayam, the party headquarters, in the evening. There was no dearth of news.

And then the Sethusamudram project hit the headlines. Tamil Nadu and Karunanidhi were hogging the limelight. As Hindu outfits howled over the project, demanding an alternative route to the proposed shipping canal in the strip of sea between Sri Lanka and India, the atheist DMK, in alliance with the Congress-led United Progressive Alliance (UPA) at the Centre, stood firm. Then Janata Party chief Subramanian Swamy, the Hindu Munnani's Ramagopalan, and others took the project to court. Their argument was that the proposed alignment for the project would mean destroying the Ramar Sethu – Adam's Bridge – the mythical bridge built by an army of monkeys for Lord Rama to wage war with Lanka and bring home his abducted wife Seetha. This, they argued, would hurt the sentiments of Hindus.

Karunanidhi was undeterred. He would say that Rama was a lie and a drunkard.[1] The Hindu outfits would froth at the mouth. He would say that Ravanan, the kidnapper of Seetha and the king of Lanka, was a 'Dravidian hero', a good man.[2] More frothing. He would refer to the Ramar Sethu as Adam's Bridge, pooh-poohing mythology and Hindu religious sentiments. Froth boiled over. All to no avail.

Ally Congress, worried that the Sethusamudram issue would hurt Hindu sentiments elsewhere in the country, began to back off, adopting a pacifist tone. Karunanidhi only became more belligerent, upping the pressure on the Centre to implement the project. A bandh call was given by all parties in Tamil Nadu in late September 2007 to demand the immediate implementation of the project. And then the Supreme Court termed the planned 1 October bandh illegal.

When CNN-IBN's Supreme Court correspondent Ashok Bagriya conveyed the developments on email, I was excited. Here was a chance to redeem myself in the eyes of my boss Radhakrishnan Nair in Delhi. The wounds of a screaming the week before were still fresh in my sensitive mind.

At a regular press briefing in the chief minister's chambers in the Secretariat the previous week, a popular English news channel's Chennai correspondent had played a dirty game. While all Tamil channels had placed their microphones on the chief minister's table, this correspondent kept hers at a slightly elevated level. Their video journalist framed it in such a way as to seem as if only their channel was present at what was in fact a press conference. The channel thus aired as 'Exclusive' a regular press briefing by the chief minister on the Sethusamudram ruckus.

Radhakrishnan Nair was quick to call and yell. 'But sir...' was all I was able to get in edgeways. I was not given a chance to explain. 'I don't know how you are going to do it but get me an exclusive interview with him immediately,' he said and hung up, leaving me furious at the injustice of it all.

Armed with Bagriya's information about the Supreme Court terming the bandh illegal, I called the chief minister's private secretary. There were two of them – Marudhanayagam was ill-tempered and prone to be rude to young reporters. Shanmuganathan was even worse. I took a chance and called the latter.

'Sir, the Supreme Court has termed the bandh illegal just now and stated that it will not be allowed,' I told him. 'Please tell Ayya (respectful term in Tamil for an elder male) I would like to know what he says,' I pleaded. Shanmuganathan was almost as powerful as Karunanidhi at the time.

'Appadiya,' he said. Is that so? 'Irunga.' Wait. I strained to listen to the whispers wafting over the phone as Shanmuganathan conveyed the message to the chief minister.

'Oru nimisham, Ayya pesanumaam,' he said. One minute, Ayya wants to speak. Before I could recover from the shock came the all-too-familiar voice rasping over the phone. 'Ahn, enna sonnaanga?' asked Karunanidhi. Yes, what did they say?

Frozen and stammering, I repeated the message from Bagriya to the chief minister of my state, all the while frantically using sign language to convey to my colleague Satish that Karunanidhi was on the line. I suddenly remembered the speaker phone option and switched it on. Satish had a light-bulb moment and began recording the audio on his phone.

Silence for just over five seconds. 'Appadina naaney unnavirathathula utkaararen,' he said. Then I will sit on hunger strike myself.

Regaining my wits somewhat, I begged him to give me a byte on camera as I was employed with a television channel. 'CIT Colony-kku vaanga, naalu mani,' he said and the line was snapped. Come to CIT Colony, 4 p.m.

Satish was a lot more excited than I. I was worried about a few things. One, my Tamil, which tended to be peppered with English. Karunanidhi was notorious for ridiculing those who did not speak fluent Tamil. Two, the NDTV office was a stone's throw from Karunanidhi's CIT Colony residence. I wanted a real exclusive.

And so we waited in silence in the street next to the chief minister's residence, removing the 'Press' sticker from the car and ducking every time a vehicle passed by. As the designated time arrived, we sprinted to the gates of the house. The security guards were aware of our appointment, thanks to Shanmuganathan. We were ushered into a large empty hall. A lone chair was placed at the centre of the hall. Karunanidhi arrived and asked us to begin.

We looked around uneasily, hesitant to ask for another chair on which I could sit and begin the questioning. He waited, yellow shawl in place, the dark glasses giving no hint of what was going on in his mind. Dressed in his usual starched white shirt and white veshti, the chief minister sat patiently, his assistant of many decades bossing us around, asking us to hurry up.

Left with no choice, I knelt down and extended the microphone to him, asking him the questions I had rehearsed in Tamil in my mind. 'If the Supreme Court has banned the bandh, I will personally sit on hunger strike,' he said. The message was powerful. It was classic Karunanidhi. He would never openly defy the highest court of law. But he would show his muscle. And it was all I needed to redeem myself.

*

I have met Karunanidhi many times since – at press meets, in the chief minister's chambers, outside the assembly, at the party headquarters and at various events. My impression of him has always been the same. A powerful man of extreme intelligence. An intelligence that could be ruthless in putting down foes. For most of his political career, an intelligence that would try to do good by the state of his birth. But also an intelligence tolerant of the faults of his loved ones and sometimes put to ill use.

The precocious and beloved son of a farmer couple, born in 1923 in the tiny village of Thirukuvalai, now in the fertile Tiruvarur district of Tamil Nadu, part of the rice bowl of India, Muthuvel Karunanidhi displayed extraordinary wit and intellect from an early age. Joining the Dravidian Self Respect movement begun by Periyar in the 1940s as a school student, Karunanidhi was noticed by its leaders for his organizational skills, his command over the Tamil language and his commitment to the ideology. A film scriptwriter by profession, Karunanidhi would wield his mighty pen to use the medium of cinema as a propaganda machine and help the Dravidian movement's ideology permeate to every village in the state.

Karunanidhi's biggest weapon would be his searing wit that spared none. An example of this is an incident in 2009, when he hit the campaign trail for the Lok Sabha polls in Rameswaram in May that year. Within a few days, he suffered severe breathing difficulties, high fever and back pain, and had to be airlifted to Chennai for hospitalization.

'I was with him when the paramedics were lifting him into the ambulance,' recalls A. Raja, former telecom minister and a leader of the DMK. 'The paramedics told him – Ayya moochcha izhutthu vidunga.' Sir, take a deep breath and then let it out. Karunanidhi caught on to the reference to 'expiration' and was quick to display his wit. 'In that state of pain and poor health, Thalaivar said – Yov, naan vida koodaadhu-nnu thaaney ya inga vandhirukken,' says Raja, rocking with laughter. You fellow, I have come here so as not to expire.

Tough questions from journalists at press conferences would often be deflected with witticisms. When asked about the timing of a particular move of his, he once replied – the time is 7 p.m. The laughter that erupted ensured that the question was neither repeated nor answered. It was also this wit that Karunanidhi would use with great skill to bargain with allies, whether the Congress or the National Democratic Alliance (NDA). His ability to bargain for plum posts in the most cut-throat manner and yet remain warm and friendly towards the leaders of national parties, cutting across ideological leanings, stood him in good stead throughout his political career.

His admiration of women is also well known. After his first wife Padmavathi passed away, Karunanidhi married Dayalu

Ammal. A relationship with Rajathi Ammal would end in a pregnancy. When he was cornered in the state assembly in 1968 and asked who Rajathi Ammal was, Karunanidhi did not bat an eyelid. 'She is my daughter Kanimozhi's mother,' he would say. Although the corridors of power in Chennai resonate with whispers about his alleged dalliances, Karunanidhi has always made it clear that his family has been his wealth. He has been accused of playing his sons M.K. Stalin and M.K. Alagiri against one another, but he has always stood like a rock by his family. Daughter Kanimozhi, often referred to as the 'literary heir' to Karunanidhi, holds a special place in his heart.

Karunanidhi is wily – truly the Chanakya of not just Tamil politics but also Indian politics. When politics required him to bend, he could and would. When politics required him to take a strident, unbending stand, that too would be accomplished with panache. The large, dentured smile, trademark dark glasses and yellow shawl arc omnipresent in Tamil Nadu – banners are unmissable, posters adorn walls, the rising sun election symbol of the DMK is painted on the mud walls of huts in the most remote corners of the state. Thalaivar – leader – to his partymen, Kalaignar – artist – to his political peers, Thatha – grandfather – to the younger generation of Tamils, Karunanidhi is closely identified with Tamil Nadu itself.

Karunanidhi may have faced condescension from the Indian English media but he has always been loved by the Tamil media. The English media looks down on him as a crass local leader who does not speak any language other than Tamil. His strident demands for state autonomy in the 1970s and 1980s were viewed as secessionist, fuelling more hatred. His reviling of Brahmins, his deliberate antagonism to the Hindu religious structure and his anti-Hindi stance could never endear him to the stars of English journalism in the north. Karunanidhi's rival J. Jayalalithaa of the

All India Anna Dravida Munnetra Kazhagam (AIADMK) was the darling instead. A fair beauty, charismatic and able to hold her own in English and Hindi, Karunanidhi's nemesis would get far more attention and sympathy from Delhi.

And yet it was Karunanidhi, in large part, who was instrumental in making Tamil Nadu one of the best performing states in terms of all social and economic indicators. It was under his leadership that flagship schemes were devised that were then followed by other states across the country. It was his understanding of the problems of the people on the ground that helped shape policy and address the critical issues of malnutrition, unemployment, caste inequities and women's rights.

It was also Karunanidhi who ushered in the 'freebie culture' in the state in 2006 with his promise of free colour TVs to the BPL (Below Poverty Line) populace if voted to power. In an election without a burning issue, the people gave him the mandate. Today, Tamil Nadu's economy is tottering on the brink of collapse as his rivals and successors have overdone his freebie strategy. Apart from essentials such as rice, the state now provides bizarre freebies – free gold for thaali (mangalsutra) for poor brides, free mixers and grinders, free milch cows and goats and heavily subsidized scooters for women, among others.

Karunanidhi would also earn notoriety for the structured, efficient, large-scale bribing of voters in 2009, when his elder son M.K. Alagiri implemented what is now known as the 'Thirumangalam formula' with grand success. It was reported that Rs 500 per vote distributed systematically by the DMK in the Thirumangalam by-election in Madurai won them the seat. Currency notes along with a printed rising sun symbol found their way into newspapers delivered at homes in the morning, were handed out outside temples and ceremoniously delivered door to door by the DMK cadre with folded hands, respectfully asking for votes.

There is much amusement among journalists who track Dravidian politics in Tamil Nadu over a Tamil saying – DMK kodu pohtta, AIADMK roadu pohduvaanga. This translates to – if the DMK draws a line, the AIADMK will lay a road. It means what the DMK does the AIADMK perfects.

The Thirumangalam formula was subsequently perfected by the AIADMK, and Tamil Nadu has faced the ignominy of having elections to three seats cancelled by the Election Commission of India following the seizure of large amounts of cash meant for distribution to voters, in Thanjavur, Aravakurichi and R.K. Nagar in 2016 and 2017.

It was also Karunanidhi who took an ideological stand against Indira Gandhi's Emergency in 1975, risking arrest and facing dismissal of his government. He was, in fact, the only leader in Tamil Nadu to oppose the Emergency tooth and nail.

It was Karunanidhi who led the support for the Mandal reforms. It was his clarion call that brought thousands of youth to the streets to protest the imposition of Hindi on a proud Tamil state. It was his unrelenting pressure on the Indira Gandhi and Rajiv Gandhi governments that forced India to arm and train the rebel LTTE (Liberation Tigers of Tamil Eelam) and send a peacekeeping force to Sri Lanka.

It was said that the LTTE had a free run in Tamil Nadu under the DMK, eventually resulting in the assassination of Rajiv Gandhi in May 1991.

On 3 June 2017, Karunanidhi, even in his absence, stitched together an important front, one that would take on the ideological right-wing forces in India. His ninety-third birthday was the date chosen for the leaders of all parties opposed to the BJP and its allies to come together for the first time on a public platform and stand with arms linked. Rahul Gandhi of the Congress, Nitish Kumar of the Janata Dal (United), Derek O'Brien of the Trinamool Congress, Omar Abdullah of the National Conference, Majeed Memon of the Nationalist Congress Party, Sitaram Yechury of the Communist Party of India (Marxist), and D. Raja and Sudhakar Reddy of the Communist Party of India were all present at the grand event at Chennai's YMCA Ground in Royapettah. This was the national Opposition's first show of strength since the Bharatiya Janata Party romped home with a huge majority in the Lok Sabha elections of 2014.

In their praise of Karunanidhi's commitment to social justice and equality and his unwavering support for minorities and the underprivileged, political leaders from Kashmir to Kerala were effusive. He was, in effect, their leader too, respected and admired across the country.

In all of this, Karunanidhi was literally mute. The tracheostomy tube still in his neck did not allow him to speak. Although he was helped to sit in his wheelchair and meet a few select leaders of his own party as well as Rahul Gandhi, visitors came away in grief. Their leader was not likely to lead them again. His face had taken on a dark hue due to over eight months of ill health and being bedridden. And yet he had formed the front.

Perhaps Karunanidhi would have liked to be the statesman that his mentor C.N. Annadurai was. Ambition may have stopped him just short of statesmanship and kept him a leader for life. Perhaps Karunanidhi was more adept at gamesmanship than statesmanship. But there is no doubt that in writing about the life of M. Karunanidhi, I am in fact documenting the history of post-Independence Tamil Nadu.

INTRODUCTION

Think Tamil Nadu, and images of beautiful ancient temples, the third longest coastline in India and Bharatnatyam dancers come to mind. Tamil Nadu is also the rice bowl of India, its Cauvery delta region plush with rich green paddy fields.

Tamil Nadu is the eleventh largest state in India. It has the second largest gross state domestic product (GSDP) in India, after Maharashtra, contributing $210 billion to India's $2.6 trillion economy.[1] With a projected growth rate of 7.94 per cent in 2017, it is one of the fastest growing states in the country. Over 54 per cent of Tamil Nadu is urbanized. The abject poverty seen in states such as Jharkhand and Chhattisgarh has long been eradicated from the southern state. With a per capita income of Rs 1,28,366[2] as opposed to the country's average of Rs 86,879 in 2014-15,[3] Tamil Nadu has raced ahead of most states in terms of well-being and welfare of its 72.1 million population as per the 2011 census. And this phenomenal success story features M. Karunanidhi in large part.

Ask just about anyone in Tamil Nadu and they will have a little story to tell about 'Kalaignar'. Autorickshaw drivers, agricultural labourers, small shopkeepers, lawyers or any of the 10 million cadre of the DMK, the oldest Dravidian party in the state – all have an anecdote about the old man that they have heard or personally experienced. Generations of babies have been named by him.

Karunanidhi's influence, though, is not limited to the prosperous and large state of Tamil Nadu. Five-time chief minister of the state – first in 1969 and even as recently as 2006-11 – Karunanidhi has also called the shots at the Centre as a crucial ally, both of the Congress and the BJP at different times. He has also been at the forefront of important social justice movements, welfare schemes, a champion of state autonomy and protector of Tamil. In these multiple hats that he donned lie Karunanidhi's genius and cunning.

A MOVEMENT FOR SOCIAL JUSTICE

In 1916, as the struggle against the British occupation of India was gaining ground all over the country, the seeds for a social revolution were sown in the south. In November that historic year, Sir P. Thyagarayar, Dr T.M. Nayar, Panagal Arasar and Dr Natesa Mudaliyar formed the South Indian Welfare Rights Association in what was then Madras.

The association was meant to be a pressure lobby to demand rights for south Indians of the Madras Province, a combination of the southern states which would be divided only after Independence. Magazines were launched by the Association in an effort to spread awareness among the masses.

In English, Dr Nayar edited a magazine called *Justice*. Bhaktavatchalam Pillai edited a Tamil magazine called *Dravidan*. And A.C. Parthasarathy Naidu was the editor of the Telugu counterpart *Andhra Prakashini*.

The South Indian Welfare Rights Association would slowly become the Justice Party and enter electoral politics.

In November 1920, the Montagu-Chelmsford Reforms came into effect, allowing the introduction of self-governing institutions by the British in India. Self-rule or swaraj was gradually ushered in.

The Justice Party leapt at the opportunity and decided to contest elections. Its main opposition was the Indian National Congress led by Annie Besant. Lord Willingdon, then Viceroy of India, invited Sir P. Thyagarayar to form the provincial government. He declined. The first ministry of the Madras Province was led by First Minister A. Subbarayalu Reddiar, with Panagal Arasar as the Second Minister and K.V. Reddiar as the Third Minister. The Congress's C. Rajagopalachari would be the Leader of the Assembly.

The concept of Dravida identity began to gain prominence with the rise of the Justice Party: the awareness that the southern part of the country had its roots in Dravidian nativity, as opposed to the Aryans of the north, and every aspect of life in the south – from food to language to culture – was that of the Dravidian tribes, the original inhabitants of the south.

E.V. Ramasamy Naicker, a wealthy land-owning farmer in Erode, jumped into this ideological fray for social justice to the Dravidians, with his Self-Respect Movement launched in 1926. Naicker's was a battle against the evils of the deep-rooted caste system in his land, where a minority of Brahmins held power and suppressed the masses on the basis of caste. He would drop his last name – Naicker, a caste identity – and urge everyone to do the same. Periyar (the Elder), as E.V. Ramasamy eventually came to be called, propagated atheism, arguing that the Hindu religion was at the root of the caste system and its discriminatory ways. He called for a scientific temperament among his people and equal rights for women. His clarion call was for 'suyamariyadhai' (self-respect) and 'samadharmam' (social justice).

Periyar's movement captured the imagination of young passionate students like C.N. Annadurai and later Karunanidhi. Periyar, who despised electoral politics, was eventually overridden by the emerging leaders of the Dravidian movement. From Periyar's Dravidar Kazhagam (DK) was born the Dravida Munnetra Kazhagam (DMK), the political party which would sweep, twist and turn Tamil politics on its head forever. And Karunanidhi would shine – in terms of his political acumen, cunning and passion, going on to virtually take over the party and establish it firmly as a political giant to be reckoned with in India.

'The personal appeal (of leaders such as Annadurai and Karunanidhi) cut across caste lines and drew the non-dominant communities to the DMK as well,' says V. Geetha, author and expert on the Dravidian movement. 'It is this appeal that gave the common person a kind of confidence to hold forth on politics, history and culture – in ways that you don't really see in most parts of India. You see it perhaps to an extent in Bengal, but it is so "bhadralok" in Bengal that you never see a Mondal or a Biswas say things with the same kind of alacrity as a Bhattacharjee or a Sen. Whereas here in Tamil Nadu you find almost everybody hold forth – whether right or wrong, they do so with such certainty and such self-confidence – and I think that is an important contribution of the party.'

But a large part of the 2 per cent Brahmin population of the state are wary of Karunanidhi. Old priests speak of the times of fear at the height of the Dravidian movement when brash young men roamed the streets, ridiculing, terrorizing and, in many instances, even chopping off the 'kudumi' (ponytail), a trademark of the upper-caste Iyers and Iyengars. The 'poonool' (sacred thread) of the hapless Brahmin male who was unfortunate enough to be caught by a Dravidian warrior would be cut. This was the culmination of the newfound anti-Brahmin rhetoric introduced by Periyar in the 1940s, which was at its height in the 1960s, when Karunanidhi was an important player in the state's politics, third in line to Annadurai.

'Karunanidhi was a very canny character from the beginning and came into his own only after Annadurai's death, when he became chief minister,' says Geetha. 'He was also seen as an ideologue who followed in the footsteps of Annadurai. His excellent PR in terms of managing the balance of power within the party, his very sharp sense of realities on the ground, his ability to weigh options – these were all his assets. I personally and sincerely think that he was not casteist. He also cultivated the support of bureaucrats from a wide range of backgrounds. He is known to have taken the bureaucracy seriously and given them the leeway to do good work. He also tried to balance the claim of social justice that the Dravidian movement swore by.'

Dalits, who comprise 19 per cent of the state's population as per the 2011 census,[4] have derided the Self-Respect Movement and its subsequent politicization for leaving them out. Electoral politics demands that majority constituencies be nurtured in order to gain votes and, in villages, the dominant castes such as Thevars or Gounders, often the perpetrators of violence against the minority Dalits in the area, were given more leeway than the social justice movement demanded.

'I think in the period through the 1950s and 1960s – a gestational period for the party – it was very, very important to build consensus,' explains Geetha, author of *Suyamariyadhai Samadharmam*, a deep dive into the Dravidian movement. 'They worked hard to build up a constituency of intellectuals amongst the non-Brahmins, often from soil that was unearthed in a sense. Not necessarily the more affluent sections like the Chettiars but they nurtured other sections of non-Brahmins as well. Karunanidhi himself is from a caste that is neither a major one in terms of population nor is it a dominant caste. So, I honestly think neither Annadurai nor Karunanidhi sought to nurture caste constituencies. That's fairly evident. But once you accept the logic of electoral democracy which works on caste, you don't have a choice but to have certain party men who represent the weight of such castes.'

Former editor-in-chief of the *Hindu* and now chairman of Kasturi and Sons and publisher of the newspaper, N. Ram agrees with the criticism levelled at the DMK and the AIADMK for not doing enough for Dalits. 'I think it's true that both the DMK and the AIADMK – when it came to the so-called caste clashes, when it came to the attacks on Dalits by the other communities, the Thevars and so on – tended to equate the aggressor with the victim. It was because of electoral politics. They did not intervene on the side of the victim. The Dalits were attacked but not seen as victims. They tended to treat them as caste clashes and very often the police tended to intervene on the side of the attackers. So, I think the criticism is warranted,' he says.

The backward castes, which constituted the Dravidian movement's biggest strength as well as around 70 per cent of the population, have been the biggest gainers of this movement. With the splintering of the DMK and the formation of the Anna Dravida Munnetra Kazhagam (ADMK) by M.G. Ramachandran in 1967, the support of the backward castes too split between the two.

The scheduled castes and scheduled tribes, which put together comprise 21 per cent of the state's population as per the 2011 census,[5] initially entranced by the call for social justice during the Dravidian movement, are now largely supporters of the AIADMK, with a fraction supporting Dalit parties.

A 'PROTECTOR' OF TAMIL AND TAMILS

In 1936, the Justice Party lost the provincial elections. In 1937, the first Congress government of Madras Province was formed, with Rajaji (C. Rajagopalachari) becoming the chief minister. As in the rest of the nation, the Congress government introduced compulsory Hindi education in schools.

The clarion call for Dravida Nadu intensified, as Periyar and other leaders saw this as an attempt to suppress indigenous Tamil culture and language. On 3 June 1938, the first anti-Hindi protest was led by Maraimalai Adigal in Saidapet in Chennai. Protests intensified across the state as leaders of Periyar's Self-Respect Movement fanned out across villages and towns, raising the flag of rebellion against the forcible imposition of Hindi, an Aryan language, on the Dravidian Tamils, Telugus, Kannadigas and Malayalees.

Karunanidhi, a precocious student at the time in Tiruvallur, was enamoured. The fiery speeches of 'Anjaa Nenjan' (Braveheart) Pattukottai Azhagirisamy and Annadurai – leaders of the Dravidian movement – captivated him. In his autobiography, *Nenjukku Needhi* (Justice for the Heart), he writes, 'The compelling arguments of Periyar's speeches, the bravery and courage in Azhagiri's sentences, Anna's beautiful Tamil – these mesmerized me.'[6]

By 1938, schoolboy Karunanidhi, barely fifteen years old, organized his fellow classmates and friends and led protest marches. He modified a small rickshaw-like pushcart and decorated it with the Tamil Thaai (mother) flag. A big banner was also put up on it with a picture of Rajaji stabbing the Tamil Thaai with the knife of compulsory Hindi.[7]

Karunanidhi also wrote a song that was sung in chorus by the band of young schoolkids as they roamed the streets:

> Come, everyone. We will go to war!
> We will drive back the Hindi ghost that has arrived.

This pluck inevitably helped him rise through the ranks of the Dravidar Kazhagam. He discovered early that his gift was language. Wit, clarity of thought and a firm grasp over Tamil history dominated Karunanidhi's writing – whether as editor of *Maanava Nesan* (Friend of Students), a handwritten newsletter started by him during those days in school, or as the founder of *Murasoli* (Drum roll), or as contributor to *Dravida Naadu* (Dravidian Land), a magazine started by Annadurai.

Tamil was his 'uyir moochu' (life breath) in more ways than one. It dominated his politics and his political career. Over time, as the first-generation leaders of the Dravidian movement passed away, Karunanidhi attempted to take over the mantle of the 'Protector' of Tamils worldwide.

REBELS OR TERRORISTS?

This Tamil rhetoric also led to Karunanidhi finding himself in a tough spot after the assassination of former Prime Minister Rajiv Gandhi in 1991. On 21 May 1991, as Gandhi was campaigning in Sriperumbudur near Chennai for the general elections scheduled for that year, a suicide bomber assassinated him. Dhanu, a member of the extremist LTTE group demanding the liberation of northern Sri Lanka, was the killer. Fellow LTTE members who were part of the conspiracy were on the run as a massive statewide hunt began.

Chief Minister Karunanidhi was dumbstruck, perhaps even afraid. 'He had supported the Tamil Eelam cause for two reasons – because he genuinely wanted to help the Sri Lankan Tamils and also because he realized it was a key emotive political plank in the state. He never thought or believed they would kill the prime minister of a friendly nation,' says a retired IPS officer who had worked closely with Karunanidhi during that time.

In June 1991, then Prime Minister P.V. Narasimha Rao, unhappy with the earlier Justice Verma Commission of Enquiry, set up another commission of inquiry headed by a sitting judge, Justice M.C. Jain of the Supreme Court. Better known as the Jain Commission, its report, submitted in 1992, blamed Karunanidhi and the DMK for the state not providing enough security to the prime ministerial candidate and also for being 'sympathetic' towards the LTTE.

An excerpt from the Jain Commission's report reads:

> The Intelligence Bureau summed up the situation prevailing at that time as follows:
>
> 'Exploiting Tamil ethnic sentiment against the deployment of IPKF in the Tamil areas of Sri Lanka, the LTTE also fomented hostile reaction against the Government of India and Shri Rajiv Gandhi through the rabid pro-Tamil groups and political parties in Tamil Nadu such as the DMK, the DK and the Taminadu Kamaraj National Congress led by P. Nedumaran. Frontline DMK and TNKC leaders had unleashed vituperative invectives against Shri Rajiv Gandhi, the then Prime Minister, for his alleged failure to protect the Tamils in Sri Lanka. An effigy of Shri Rajiv Gandhi was also burnt by DMK workers at Palani on October 11, 1987.
>
> A DMK leader S. Kandappan had threatened that there would be widespread bomb explosions throughout Tamil Nadu on Diwali Day in 1987, if IPKF operations did not cease by then. A procession taken out under the auspices of the Liberation Tigers Solidarity Organisation led by Ramakrishnan (DK) at Coimbatore

> on June 1, 1988, raised slogans warning that any harm done to the LTTE leader, Prabhakaran, would lead to chaos in Tamilnadu and the Congress (I) leadership including Shri Rajiv Gandhi would be attacked. The President of the Tamil Protection Federation, Tamil Mannan, held Shri Rajiv Gandhi personally responsible for the rape and murders perpetrated on Tamils in Sri Lanka by the IPKF.

It was a big blow to Karunanidhi, as the Jain Commission also categorically stated that his government had provided a safe haven to the militant outfit.

In Tamil Nadu, the DMK government came to power in January 1989. Soon after, the LTTE began expanding their bases in the state. The upswing in the LTTE activities during the DMK regime in Tamil Nadu led to:

- Establishment of at least 40 landing points all along the Tamilnadu coast;
- Maintenance of an elaborate clandestine communication network in Tamil Nadu;
- Establishment of active LTTE cadres in about 26 posts and proliferation of LTTE elements all over Tamil Nadu;
- Establishment of underground factories manufacturing arms and explosive devices.

In another threat assessment during the same period, it was acknowledged by the Intelligence Bureau in a report dated 6 April 1990, (Annexure S-64) that

> There is some information that some militant elements of the LTTE might resort to do physical harm to the former Prime Minister of India, Shri Rajiv Gandhi, and these elements seem emboldened in their hostile attitude towards the former Prime

> Minister especially after the defeat of the Congress-I Government at the Centre.
>
> It is surprising that with the vast reservoir of intelligence indicating LTTE's growing animus against Shri Rajiv Gandhi, a sensational act of terrorism by LTTE on 19th June 1990 in Madras was not perceived as a threat to Shri Rajiv Gandhi's life.

The 19 June episode referred to was the daring daylight murder of EPRLF (Eelam People's Revolutionary Liberation Front) leader Padmanabha, a breakaway faction opposing the LTTE, along with fourteen others in Kodambakkam, Chennai, where he was in hiding. This murder too was confirmed to have been carried out by the LTTE. But the perpetrators managed to escape in a Maruti car, driving all the way to Nagapattinam, hopping on to a boat and heading back to Sri Lanka two days after the crime. The Jain Commission observed: 'No investigation worth its name was conducted by the state police in this case.'

Indicted and reviled by the Congress, Karunanidhi faced a seemingly bleak future and impending arrest. But while the interim report of the Jain Commission held the DMK responsible for lax security and a pro-LTTE stand that led to Gandhi's killing, the final report absolved him and the party of any wrongdoing.

'His greatest failure was the Eelam struggle,' says Geetha. 'He got so caught up with the idea of being a Tamil saviour that he really did not realize what was actually going on. He had no sense of the ground realities in Sri Lanka. I also think he has no taste for militant politics. Maybe it was also a sense of wanting to preserve what he had stood for all his life – the idea of Tamil.'

But the politician turned the tale around – shedding his pro-LTTE politics while retaining his pro-Tamil stance and becoming an important ally of the Congress and, ironically, its next leader, Rajiv's widow, Sonia Gandhi.

RELATIONSHIP WITH THE CENTRE

The DMK's rise to a position of power at the Centre as a crucial ally for various governments began during Indira Gandhi's time.

In 1969, the Indian National Congress split over the issue of the presidential candidate. While the party had nominated Dr Neelam Sanjiva Reddy as the candidate, then Prime Minister Indira Gandhi decided to favour V.V. Giri, an independent candidate. Giri, with the help of Gandhi's machinations, became the President of India, leading to the splitting of the Congress into two factions – the Congress (O) and the Congress (R). The Congress (O) had tall leaders such as Morarji Desai, K. Kamaraj and S. Nijalingappa opposing the Congress (R) faction led by Indira Gandhi along with Jagjivan Ram and Shankar Dayal Sharma.

The DMK, under Karunanidhi, decided to ally with the Indira faction for the 1971 polls. While he supported Gandhi in decisions such as the nationalization of banks and abolition of the privy purse, Karunanidhi's was also the lone, shrill voice against the imposition of Emergency in 1975 by Gandhi. For this, his party men were arrested with brute force in the state and his son M.K. Stalin jailed and beaten mercilessly.

Karunanidhi also played a crucial role in changing central government policy in 1965 when he and Annadurai led the next wave of anti-Hindi agitations in the state. The Centre had attempted to make Hindi the sole official language of the country and the Dravidians of Tamil Nadu were incensed. The protests paid off, forcing the Centre to put the move on hold.

Tamil pride was also used by the DMK and Karunanidhi to push hard for federalism and state autonomy, in effect preventing the Centre from becoming the 'Big Brother'. The rise and might of the DMK was a springboard for regional parties across the country to emerge and make more vociferous demands for state autonomy.

In August 2007, Karunanidhi, who was chief minister at the time, wrote an article which was published in the *Hindu*. In that piece, he recalled the fight for federalism begun by Annadurai and taken over by him:

> On August 19, 1969, I announced on the floor of the Legislative Assembly the formation of a Three Member Committee with Dr. P.V. Rajamannar as Chairman and Dr. A.L. Mudaliar and P. Chandra Reddy as Members...
>
> In its 1971 Election Manifesto, the DMK announced: 'Though the Constitution of India is described as a Federal one, the balance is more tilted towards the Centre and hence the States are not able to function freely in the administrative and financial spheres. Only such powers as are necessary for the Centre to preserve the strength of India should be assigned to the Centre and all the other powers should be left to the States without impairing the ideal of a strong India.'
>
> The report of the Rajamannar Committee was received on May 27, 1971. On April 16, 1974, I moved a historic resolution in the Tamil Nadu Legislative Assembly requesting the Central government to accept the views of the Tamil Nadu government on State autonomy and the recommendations of the Rajamannar Committee and proceed to effect immediate changes in the Constitution of India to establish a truly federal set-up. In 1974, Murasoli Maran, an inimitable ideologue of the DMK, brought out a brilliant treatise on State autonomy. He explained in simple and effective language decentralisation and federalism; devolution and provincial autonomy; the nature of the Indian Constitution; and the basis for State autonomy.
>
> For the first time, in 1989, a National Front coalition government headed by V.P. Singh, which included major regional

parties like the DMK, took office at the Centre. Though short-lived, this government took certain steps to strengthen the federal principle. The Inter-State Council was constituted in 1990. The entry of regional parties in coalition governments at the Centre became a regular feature in 1996 with the formation of the United Front government and in all subsequent ones – and presently in the United Progressive Alliance government functioning under the esteemed guidance of Sonia Gandhi. The Left parties, which supported both the National Front Government in 1989 and the United Front government in 1996-1998 and the present UPA government, are strong supporters of the federal principle.[8]

The DMK also hustled to save the country from instability by aligning with the BJP-led NDA in the general elections of 1999. A year previously, the NDA had been formed with the AIADMK led by J. Jayalalithaa as part of the front. It came to power on a slim majority and lasted barely a year. Jayalalithaa, who had demanded that the Atal Bihari Vajpayee government sack the DMK government in the state – a demand which was refused – took her revenge on the coalition by withdrawing support, toppling the government.

Karunanidhi showed his political acumen. On 20 February 1999, the Left parties had organized a 'People's Convention against Communalism'. At this event, the DMK's fiery leader Murasoli Maran delivered a speech stating that the BJP's Hindutva politics was 'the biggest threat to the country'.[9] Maran made a speech characterizing the BJP as fascist or semi-fascist. Then there was a dramatic shift. The DMK joined hands with the BJP to fight the elections of 1999.

The *Hindu* group's *Frontline* magazine, in its 24 April 1999 edition, carried a scathing report on the political skullduggery of the time:

> The BJP's persuasive powers seemed to be working, up to a point, as some parties and leaders performed amazing political somersaults. The Dravida Munnetra Kazhagam (DMK), the principal opponent of the AIADMK in Tamil Nadu, 'discovered' barely 24 hours after the AIADMK formally parted ways with the BJP that the saffron party's communalism was less dangerous than the 'threat posed to the country by AIADMK leader Jayalalithaa's corruption'. Coming from a party that had been a founder-member of the National Front, the grouping of non-Congress (I), non-BJP secular parties that had spearheaded a principled campaign against the BJP brand of Hindutva communalism and identified it as the most serious threat to the secular fabric and the integrity of the country, it seemed to point to an inexplicable eagerness to clamber off the secular ideological platform for short-term political expediency.

'When we asked other leaders of the DMK, not Kalaignar, about this, they said to further the interests of the state, you must have relations with the Centre. It was opportunism, no question,' says N. Ram.

Karunanidhi moved into the NDA in Jayalalithaa's stead and, in the election of 1999, fought with the BJP. The coalition won a large majority and Vajpayee became prime minister once again, completing the full five-year term.

Karunanidhi, though, was uncomfortable in the NDA. 'He has always said that he regretted the alliance with the NDA,' says A. Raja, former telecom minister and a leader of the DMK. 'This was mainly because of the chaos of the Babri Masjid demolition and other such things they did during that period.'

Karunanidhi locked horns with the NDA on the issues of building a Ram temple in Ayodhya, demolition of the Babri Masjid, the BJP's call for a uniform civil code and other such moves that he perceived as detrimental to minority religions in the country. In 2003, he stated firmly to media persons: 'We will continue to oppose any move for a temple project at the disputed site in Ayodhya. If they (the BJP) resent our opposition and show us the door, then we are ready to quit the NDA.' Karunanidhi reiterated with increasing emphasis that building a Ram temple at the disputed site in Ayodhya would lead to 'dangerous consequences'.[10]

By 2004, Karunanidhi worked his way back into the Congress's UPA coalition, never going back to the NDA again. 'He was a key architect of the United Progressive Alliance in 2004, despite being with the BJP for quite a while,' says N. Ram.

Karunanidhi also played a crucial role in the support for and implementation of the Mandal Commission reforms, providing reservations on the basis of caste in the country. A staunch supporter of the reforms introduced by the V.P. Singh government at the Centre in 1990, it was the DMK's support under Karunanidhi that softened the anger amongst the forward castes in Tamil Nadu.

'The emergence of the social justice platform at the national level under V.P. Singh – I think it was the DMK's presence, which lasted for two years, 1989 to '91, that made the politics of the United Front possess a certain contemporary resonance,' says V. Geetha. 'For many of us the Mandal reforms forced us to think of caste in a different way. In a more popular sense, though, Karunanidhi made the issue relevant, telling Tamilians what was the legacy they should value and reminded them of their history and culture. So much so that Jayalalithaa would be forced to extend it [the reservation quota] to 61 per cent.'

WELFARE AND POPULISM

What was begun by Kamaraj as Congress chief minister between 1954 and 1967 was taken forward by the DMK governments under Annadurai from 1967 onwards when the party came to power. Following Anna's untimely death in 1969, Karunanidhi became chief minister and continued the tradition of welfare and populist schemes that eventually helped Tamil Nadu rise in all socio-economic indicators.

Kamaraj had initiated the mid-day meal scheme, a pioneering scheme in the country to get children from poor socio-economic backgrounds to school. One nutritious meal a day – lunch – was served to all children studying in government schools. This was a resounding success, bringing poor children from the marginalized castes into an educational system which was thus far denied them.

Kamaraj also began schemes to provide scholarships to Dalit students so that they could get a good education. 'We shouldn't forget that Kamaraj had the explicit support of Periyar through his term in office, largely because Periyar saw in Kamaraj a very astute politician who would answer the call of social justice through specific legislative and other kinds of actions,' says Geetha. 'So in terms of governance itself, whether it was the mid-day meal scheme or his role in ensuring that schools were seen as open spaces, giving support to what was called in those days the "Harijan" population – Kamaraj laid the foundation for a durable, workable political and populist kind of approach to education and social welfare.'

Karunanidhi worked on that foundation and made it better. 'Nobody could ignore it since it was so weighty in nature. So I think the subsequent governments that came extended these policies more and more – to a point where they became so populist that they eventually sank the state. In that sense, Karunanidhi had to continue – he couldn't roll anything back and I think it was not in his interest to roll anything back,' she adds.

'I think it's made a difference. Some of it has been wasted – we can't say there has been no corruption. But it has made a difference. The mid-day meal scheme and the universal PDS [public distribution system] are really worth highlighting. They have not compromised on coverage, and even though there is an element of corruption, I think these are well administered and well monitored,' says N. Ram.

Housing schemes were announced for the urban poor, providing accommodation for them at reasonable rates and, many times, free of cost. Karunanidhi also nationalized bus transportation in the state, improving connectivity and making it affordable for the poorest sections of the populace.

'I think among his sharper and more intuitive policies was the one to nationalize transport, which I think achieved for Tamil Nadu what other states could not – connecting schools, markets. In terms of governance, there were some major decisions taken by Karunanidhi that helped the state,' says Geetha.

Karunanidhi is also known for being a 'people's chief minister'. The doors to his house and his office in the Secretariat when he was chief minister were always open to the public. He consciously cultivated the perception of accessibility and approachability, a trait that no politician in the state has been able to develop since.

'His choices were, ultimately, not very different from those of most other politicians before him, in terms of cultivating caste constituencies or staying with populist and neo-liberal policies for electoral gains – all of that cannot be vastly different in any case,' says Geetha. 'The difference was in terms of how he managed inter-state relations, communicating with the constituency, and not really being very democratic in a very deep manner but still managing to create the impression of openness.'

Eventually, competitive electoral politics forced Karunanidhi to take the freebie culture one step further than his successor M.G. Ramachandran. In 2006, Karunanidhi, faced with an election without any major issue, swung the tide in his favour with a masterstroke – free colour televisions for BPL families in the state. In response, his rival Jayalalithaa, in 2011, offered free mixers and grinders, laptops for students and other kinds of ridiculous freebies, causing the burden on the state exchequer to balloon to unimaginable proportions.

'SCIENTIFIC CORRUPTION'

As nation-building began in earnest in the late 1950s and 1960s, so did infrastructure development in the form of highways, laying of roads, dams and reservoirs. Charges of corruption in these works involving the DMK slowly surfaced.

The term 'scientific corruption' was made famous during the hearings of the Sarkaria Commission of Inquiry appointed by the Centre to probe charges of corruption by then Chief Minister M. Karunanidhi and the DMK government in the construction of flyovers, the Veeranam dam in Cuddalore and other similar projects.

The commission was set up on the basis of a letter by M.G. Ramachandran along with other leaders of the AIADMK to the President of India, detailing various allegations of illegality by the then DMK regime. In February 1976 the Centre set up the Commission of Inquiry headed by R.S. Sarkaria, a sitting judge of the Supreme Court.

The final report of the Sarkaria Commission in 1976 was damning. It stated that Karunanidhi as chief minister had abused his office of power to favour those close to him. The report reluctantly stated, though, that there was not enough evidence to actually prosecute him.

A key extract from the final report states:

> It has been established that Shri. Karunanidhi, abusing his official position as Chief Minister, actuated with the motive to unduly favour Sathyanarayana Brothers with the award of the contract for the Veeranam project, directed the Chief Engineer, Shri. Hussain, to tailor his recommendations on the tenders in such a manner as would enable the Government to accept the tender of Sathyanarayana Bros...
>
> There is no doubt that Shri. Karunanidhi was interested in the contract being given to Sathyanarayana Bros. for some extraneous consideration. In this connection two circumstances have been firmly established: 1. Purushothaman's friendship with Maran and his exploiting this friendship to influence Karunanidhi and through him, Hussain; 2. The supply of materials worth about Rs. 59,202 by Purushothaman for construction of 'Murasoli building' without accepting payment – a fact admitted by Maran himself.
>
> With regard to the alleged payment of illegal gratification of Rs. 29 lakhs in seven installments by Purushothaman to Karunanidhi, the story of Purushothaman is not such that it can be rejected breevi manu. But as he is admitted an accomplice, his evidence cannot be acted upon without corroboration in material particulars by independent evidence. The corroboration available is not adequate in extent and specificity and this evidence on record goes no further than establishing a preponderance of possibility, coming perilously close to probability, in favour of this charge. The charge of accepting illegal gratification has thus not been indubitably established against Shri. Karunanidhi.

> Public money to the extent of nearly Rs. 6 crores was squandered over this project and as rightly pointed out in the report of the Technical committee set up by the State Government, the project cannot now be brought to its successful conclusion, unless the foreign collaborators, M/S Vacrete, accept full responsibility for the manufacture, testing, laying and jointing of pipes.
>
> To the public exchequer, it would mean an additional burden of several crores and to the public looking long for adequate water supply, a tortuous wait for at least two years more. The responsibility for this huge waste of public money must rest squarely on Shri Karunanidhi and Shri Sadiq Pasha.[11]

Karunanidhi alleged a witch-hunt by MGR and went to court pleading for dismissal of the Commission of Inquiry. '... allegations were made in 1972, a by-election intervened and the party (AIADMK) came out successful with huge majority,' said Karunanidhi in his 1977 petition before the Madras High Court. He also pointed to a two-year delay between the allegations and the actual inquiry, arguing that it was spurred on by politics.

The petition was dismissed. But the term stuck. 'Scientific corruption' became a slogan of sorts for the rival AIADMK and Jayalalithaa to attack Karunanidhi with over the years.

Many allegations of corruption have been raised against Karunanidhi and his ministers since then. But as far as Karunanidhi was concerned, nothing ever stuck.

From 2007 onwards, the DMK slowly got embroiled in the 2G spectrum scandal, the allegation being that DMK MP and then Telecom Minister A. Raja had received kickbacks for allocating spectrum for telecom operators. The Comptroller and Auditor General (CAG) of India, in 2010, released its report damning the telecom minister. The report stated that his move to refuse the auction of spectrum had caused a loss of Rs 1.76 lakh crore to the exchequer. The trial court in Delhi eventually acquitted all the accused in the 2G case, even as the CBI prepared to go on appeal.

At the time, though, Karunanidhi's daughter Kanimozhi, a Rajya Sabha MP herself, also became involved in the scam. A Rs 200 crore loan from one of the companies that received spectrum was given to the DMK-owned Kalaignar TV, in which Kanimozhi was a director. While Karunanidhi vigorously supported both A. Raja and his daughter, claiming that they did no wrong, both were incarcerated in Tihar Jail – Kanimozhi for some months and Raja for over a year.

The Manmohan Singh government at the Centre, with which the DMK was in alliance at the time, fought bravely. Kapil Sibal, then minister and a spokesperson of the Congress, stated that the '2G controversy was only a notional loss and not an actual one'.

But relations ultimately soured between the Congress and DMK as international disrepute set in, and Raja was forced to resign. In 2011, *Time* magazine put the 2G scam at number two in its international list of 'Top Ten Abuses of Power 2011'.[12]

But Karunanidhi chugged right along. Battling feuds within his large family, feuds within his party as well as the rising might of the AIADMK under Jayalalithaa, Karunanidhi continued to be unfazed.

Nevertheless, the 2G controversy as well as allegations of land grabbing by DMK party workers and leaders during his last regime between 2006 and 2011 put paid to the DMK's electoral chances. The AIADMK led by a resurgent Jayalalithaa swept the state polls in 2011 with a brute majority and came back for a second consecutive term in 2016.

Soon after the elections that year, Jayalalithaa fell ill and was hospitalized for seventy-five days from 21 September, breathing her last after a massive cardiac arrest on 5 December. In the meanwhile, Karunanidhi too fell ill, was hospitalized intermittently and his health has deteriorated slowly. He lost his power of speech and has had fewer and fewer lucid moments.

With both arch rivals suddenly out of the political scene, Tamil Nadu politics has been thrown into chaos and various wolves have taken over.

1

EARLY YEARS

How does one document the early years of a leader who has been in public life for sixty years and who has outlived almost all of his contemporaries? Karunanidhi himself provides the answer.

His voracious appetite for the written word and an elephantine memory gifts the Tamil reader with a mass of literature and oratory to piece together details of those tumultuous and extraordinary pre-Independence years when Karunanidhi was a schoolboy. His followers have done the rest – regularly compiling and releasing 'malars' or little magazines on Kalaignar-based themes – his witticisms, his speeches in the Assembly, chronicles of his life and his political speeches. This material is preserved at Kalaignar Karuvoolam, a library-cum-bookstore located within the premises of the DMK party headquarters in Chennai, Anna Arivalayam.

Karunanidhi's love for the written word perhaps stems from the nature of the Dravidian movement itself. In the 1940s, when television and radio were unknown, it was pamphlets, magazines, public meetings and street theatre that helped spread the ideology of self-respect and social justice. Voluminous material was written and distributed to every nook and corner of the state as small magazines sprouted, carrying in writing the spoken words of Periyar, Annadurai and other key leaders of the Dravidian movement.

Karunanidhi began his autobiography in 1975. Called *Nenjukku Needhi* (Justice for the Heart), its five volumes cover in great detail his life and experiences until 2002. Even during his stints in between this period as chief minister, Karunanidhi continued to write.

'Writing was like yoga for him,' recalls N. Ram. 'He wrote every day.'

Nenjukku Needhi begins with a narrative of how he managed to write voluminously over the years. Karunanidhi states that ever since he became a minister, 'the time I get to write my poetry is mostly while in a train'.[1]

He gives a lyrical description of the mild subterfuge involved in indulging in this love. 'After 10 p.m., once the carriage doors are shut, I pretend to sleep. After that one believes that the onlookers, the petitioners are definitely not around. Even then, at some stops, some people bang on the doors and say – "Oh you poor man, it seems we woke you up when you were in deep sleep. It is all right, do excuse us" – and they smile at you. In the midst of all this, once the satisfaction of having written twenty or thirty pages sets in, I sleep at 5 a.m., wake up at 6 a.m. at my destination – there is a special joy in all of this.'[2]

A FATHER'S BELOVED SON

In the late 1800s, or the early 1900s perhaps, a young couple, Ayyathurai and Periyanaayagathammal, in the little village of

Thirukuvalai in Madras Presidency's Tiruvarur area, was over the moon. Periyanaayagathammal was heavy with child. 'In his happiness that his companion would become a mother and he a father, Ayyathurai did pujas at all big temples and to all small goddesses.'[3]

The baby, a beautiful boy, was born. But his mother died a week after. Two months later, father Ayyathurai too died of grief. 'Having lost both of them, and uncaring, the tender infant lay.'[4]

'In those days there was no dearth of love in Thirukuvalai... Thillaiammal and Meenatchi [other residents of the village] took on the responsibility of raising that child...On their shoulders and in their laps, the baby grew up with no two days or moments alike. Either because of the joy of having found a pearl or because the pearl was the cause of the death of its oyster – the baby was named Muthuvel. That baby was my father,' writes Karunanidhi.

Muthuvel is a combination of two words – 'muthu' meaning pearl and 'vel' referring to the spear carried by Lord Murugan, son of Shiva, a popular deity in Tamil Nadu.

In Tamil Nadu, the father's name is a prefix to the given name, many times simply as an initial. Ayyathurai Muthuvel grew up an orphan with two mothers, seemingly demonstrating an irreverence for societal hierarchies and mores, while being immensely God-fearing. A farmer, neither wealthy nor poor, he belonged to the Isai Vellalar caste, a community with a minuscule population in the state, which traditionally played musical instruments at the homes of people of other castes during functions and deaths.

Muthuvel was precocious, mocking and well-versed in Sanskrit. 'He would recite the Mahabharata and Ramayana better than the pundits,' according to Karunanidhi.[5]

Muthuvel demonstrated his inclination to poetry and song, singing aloud his own compositions on local scandals, much to the consternation of the other residents of Thirukuvalai. A scandal that wagged many tongues in Muthuvel's younger years related to a rich landlord's young wife and her lurid multiple affairs. Her rendezvous with her lovers would take place near the temple in the village and the tales eventually found their way to the ears of her much older and hapless husband. This captured Muthuvel's imagination, spurring him to write a song, punning on God and temple, and with a hint of feminism in his creation.

So what if the neighbours see
So what if they call it indignity
So what if the whole mandal knows
So what if respect – and marriage – goes?

Having tied the thaali (mangalsutra) on the advice of your mother
You left, having fallen in love with another
You are led astray thinking that women are goddesses
And you embroil yourself in the wrong culture.

Despite your having your own village
Despite your being at the helm of affairs in your home
Despite your having your own eateries and buildings,
You went inside God's own home.

You saw the debauchery with your own eyes
Hurriedly gathering her clothes
Feasted fully on the nectar in the pot
Hurriedly jumped over the low wall and ran.

From there I went to the kannimoolai (meaning southwest, punning on virginity) room

> I saw the handsome Velappasamy (pun on the name of the deity as her lover)
> I united with him and returned.
>
> Who can I tell about the wonder there?
> Ammamma, you hear me.[6]

Muthuvel found an enamoured young woman who insisted that she would marry only him and none other. Kunjammal became his wife. After her death within the first few years of marriage, Kunjammal became a sorrowful Muthuvel's 'kuladeivam' (deity of the clan). Her bangles and wedding garlands were stashed away in a small box and worshipped in his home. Muthuvel married again, but Vedammal too died soon after.

His third wife, Anjugam, gave him his heirs – two daughters, Periyanayagam, named after her paternal grandmother, and Shanmugasundarathammal. At long last, the much-awaited son was born on 3 June 1924. Muthuvel Karunanidhi was the apple of everyone's eye.

A TASTE OF CASTE REPRESSION

The proud father had decided that Karunanidhi would have what he himself lacked – a sound education and training in music. Upon returning from school, the young Karunanidhi would be forced to take lessons from a tutor who came home. 'But I was not enthralled by music lessons,' recalls Karunanidhi in his book.[7]

The young mind revolted against the caste-based discrimination that he was continually subjected to in Thirukuvalai. 'In front of the "big" men we could not wear shirts. We had to tie the upper cloth around our waist. It was wrong to wear slippers. Such was the vicious repression in those days,' he writes. 'In the name of God, in the name of caste and religious rituals, one community was perpetrating torture, and my young mind began to oppose it heartily.'

High school beckoned, and as Thirukuvalai did not offer higher education, it was decided to send Karunanidhi to the town of Tiruvarur to pursue his studies. At the age of twelve, in 1936, Karunanidhi and his father Muthuvel, along with a neighbour, went to the Tiruvarur high school, and Karunanidhi wrote the entrance exams, confident of securing admission. They were in for a rude shock.

'The headmaster of the high school said that I was not fit to even join the fifth standard,' recounts Karunanidhi. His name was Kasturi Iyengar.

Muthuvel was shattered. But his son did not take no for an answer. Bursting unannounced into the headmaster's room, with a peon chasing him, Karunanidhi made a desperate argument. 'If I go back to my village, everyone will laugh at me.' Headmaster Iyengar reiterated a firm no. 'In that case, I will jump into the lake in front of your eyes and die.' With this statement, the twelve-year-old burst into uncontrollable sobs.

Iyengar relented and Karunanidhi secured admission in the fifth standard. He stood first in class that year.

INTRODUCTION TO POLITICAL THOUGHT

It was a fifty-page book in Tamil, part of the syllabus, titled *Panagal Arasar* that caught the teenager's fancy. Karunanidhi remembers that only he in the entire class knew that book by heart. This was his introduction to politics and political thought.

Panagal Arasar was one of the founders of the Justice Party, which many see as the precursor to the DMK. With Periyar's launch of the Self-Respect Movement in 1926, students across the state were captivated – one of them, C.N. Annadurai, studying in Madras's Pachaiyappa's College, began to be noticed as a firebrand orator as he debated on the movement and its ideology. In 1930, Annadurai formed the Self-Respect Youth Body in the college.

When Karunanidhi joined the fifth standard in Tiruvarur, the Justice Party lost the election. The next year, the first Congress government was elected in Madras, defeating the Swarajya Party. Rajaji became the chief minister and ushered in a law to make the learning of Hindi in schools compulsory.

There was furore among the intelligentsia of the state. Periyar and his followers raised the flag of rebellion against the imposition of Hindi on a Dravidian populace. Meetings, marches, pamphlets and magazines were distributed by the followers of Periyar's ideology, urging the people to oppose Hindi.

On 3 June 1938, the first anti-Hindi protest was held in Saidapet, Madras, led by Maraimalai Adigal. Pattukottai Azhagirisamy, the 'suraavali pechaalar' (whirlwind speaker) of the Self-Respect Movement, led a march all over the state in protest against the imposition of Hindi.

Karunanidhi devoured the developments keenly and was roused. 'The compelling arguments of Periyar's speeches, the bravery and courage in Azhagiri's sentences, Anna's beautiful Tamil – these mesmerized me,' he writes.[8]

Such was the impression made by Azhagirisamy on the young Karunanidhi that many years later he would name his son after him. Of course, M.K. Azhagiri's followers did the obvious – they gave him the moniker of 'Anjaa Nenjan' or Braveheart, the same as for Pattukottai Azhagirisamy.

By 1938, at the age of fourteen, Karunanidhi had cobbled together a band of boys as well as a cycle rickshaw. This ragged gang roamed the streets of Tiruvarur with the Tamil Thaai (Tamil mother) flag perched on a pole atop the vehicle. A picture of Rajaji stabbing the Tamil Thaai with the dagger of compulsory Hindi was soon added to the melee. Karunanidhi composed little ditties that his gang shouted as they went along.

On one of those rounds, his Hindi teacher from school was witness to these protests. Karunanidhi went up to the teacher, handed him a pamphlet and shouted in his face, 'Defeat Hindi! Long live Tamil!' The teacher did not say a word. 'But an answer awaited me the next day in class,' writes Karunanidhi.[9]

> On the classroom's blackboard, he (the Hindi teacher) wrote some Hindi words. He asked me to read them. I stood up.
>
> 'Mmm…Let me see you read,' he said.
>
> I could read only if I understood! So I stood silent as he approached. The class looked on with great expectation. The teacher twisted my ear.
>
> 'Can you read or not?' he growled.
>
> 'I don't understand,' I told him. He slapped me hard on my cheek. The classroom spun along with my head. I managed to sit down.[10]

Nevertheless, his protests continued. Karunanidhi participated in debates and honed his oratorical skills in school. The first such debate did not come easy. The topic was friendship. Karunanidhi told a beautifully woven story of the lasting friendship between Duryodhana and Karnan in the Mahabharata. The speech won him laurels. But Karunanidhi confesses, 'How would they know that for three days I wrote and memorized and spoke to pillars in my home.'

When he was fifteen years old, Karunanidhi first put his writing skills on display. He founded a fortnightly magazine for students called *Manava Nesan* (Friend of Students). The manuscripts were handwritten and fifty copies were made by hand and distributed by him and his friends.[11]

The first tryst with politics came in the form of a communist cadre dressed in a khadi shirt and dark glasses who had sought him out. Perhaps expecting to find someone older, the man asked doubtfully, 'Are you the same Karunanidhi who is writing *Manava Nesan*?'

The communist told Karunanidhi to bring students from the schools of Tiruvarur together to further a cause – the clarion call was for freedom, tolerance and equality. He also encouraged him to begin a weekly tabloid. Four months after this meeting, *Murasoli* (Drum roll) was founded.

Enthused by the communist's interest and advice, Karunanidhi brought together 200 students and the khadi-clad man conducted elections. Karunanidhi became the secretary of the student group, while his friend S.P. Chidambaram was made the treasurer. Students affiliated to the Congress party too joined the group and began suggesting that a slogan be raised: 'Long live Tamil! Let Hindi grow!' Students affiliated to the communists nodded in agreement. Karunanidhi refused to acquiesce. Having spent a sleepless night, Karunanidhi decided that he wanted no truck with the communists or the Congress. He decided to dissolve the association.

'I returned Rs 100 to the students from the fees collected. Some of them refused to take the money. Using that, I started the Tamil Students' Association [in 1941],' writes Karunanidhi. After that, he never saw the communist. Karunanidhi was firmly on the path towards Periyar and Anna.

Those close to Karunanidhi vouch for the many times he has said that if he had not followed Periyar and Anna, he would have been a communist instead. Engaged deeply in the Dravidian movement by now, Karunanidhi had little time to attend school. He failed thrice in his final year. As a fourth attempt was not allowed, he had little choice. He left schooling behind.

By 1939, Rajaji's term as chief minister came to an end. An interim government took over and rescinded the compulsory Hindi legislation. This was the first victory for the anti-Hindi protesters.

IMMERSION IN POLITICS

The interest in politics which began when he was merely fourteen years old grew as he got closer to his twentieth year. In 1942, C.N. Annadurai started a magazine called *Dravida Nadu*. An eager Karunanidhi was desperate to write for it. Having asked around and not being able to find an address to send his submission to, Karunanidhi simply posted it to 'Dravida Nadu, Kanchipuram'. Miraculously, his article was published under the title 'Ilamai Bali' (Sacrifice of Youth) the very next week. He writes that he was overjoyed. 'Until then, only four or five people would read my work. Now, hundreds, thousands would read.'[12]

Two weeks later, Annadurai visited Tiruvarur for a function on Nabigal Naayagam, an Islamic ritual. This was the first time the mentor and the protégé would meet. 'Who is Karunanidhi in this town?' asked Anna. 'Please bring him, I want to meet him.'

Karunanidhi recalls that Anna was stunned when he looked at him. 'Are you studying?' he asked Karunanidhi. In a trembling voice came the response – 'Yes I am.' Anna's response threw the young boy: 'Hereafter do not send me any articles.'[13]

Although the two would become closer than blood brothers over the years, Karunanidhi was shattered at that first meeting. To give vent to his literary urge, he began to write and stage dramas in Tiruvarur that propagated and publicized the ideology of the Dravidian movement.

It was a time of turbulence. Karunanidhi had little money. Loans were taken to stage plays but the returns often did not cover the cost of the play itself. The resourcefulness of the young, upcoming politician was honed as he went about with a firm resolve to stage the plays at any cost – by begging for loans, selling any old item in his possession or charming a rich man into paying for the drama.

The year 1944 marked a turning point in the Dravidian movement, as Periyar, as the leader of the Justice Party, changed its name to Dravidar Kazhagam (DK). In the conference of the Justice Party held at Salem, he also announced that the DK would never enter electoral politics. Two important resolutions were also passed at that conference – one stating that all non-Brahmins should give up any title or honour conferred upon them by the British, and the other demanding a separate electorate for the scheduled castes.

The DK's Tamil mouthpiece, the magazine *Kudiyarasu* (Republic), records a meeting between B.R. Ambedkar and Periyar in which the former is said to have endorsed the latter's resolutions and views.

In October 1944 was planned a large public meeting in Chidambaram, near Cuddalore. The rally was called the Varnaashrama Maanadu (Varnaashrama Meeting). For the Periyarists, this was anathema. Karunanidhi launched a scathing attack on the meeting in his own journal *Murasoli*, exhorting people to come in droves to protest against the Chidambaram meeting.

In *Nenjukku Needhi*, he recaptures a sense of that glorious exhilarating time of rebellion.

In our glorious state
Which has sung the song of many victories
Without a bit of shame
Some selfish brethren come together
And even if they turn somersaults in a vain effort
To set down the roots of varnam (caste)
Protect your self-respect
Upon pain of death, brave Tamizhaa!
Fight!
Down with Varnaashramam![14]

In an undated public meeting in which 'Anjaa Nenjan' Pattukottai Azhagirisamy spoke, a rapt Karunanidhi watched him hold forth with brilliance for well over an hour. To his shock, Azhagirisamy collapsed on stage, writhing in pain. Someone told Karunanidhi that 'Anjaa Nenjan' was a 'noyaali' (ill, a patient). Karunanidhi recalls asking that person why then did he shout in such a fashion.

Azhagirisamy heard Karunanidhi and told him, 'Thambi (younger brother), this country is more diseased than I am. If a doctor has a cold, can he refuse to treat someone with a fever? That is how I work,' he told the young boy. These words of the braveheart made a lasting impression on Karunanidhi. 'I became a slave to Azhagiri's "kolgai veri" (ideological fanaticism),' he writes.[15]

MARRIAGE AND CHILD

In the midst of the writing, oratory at local meetings, staging of plays and complete immersion in the Dravidar Kazhagam, Karunanidhi's family decided that it was time for him to get married. The hunt for a suitable bride began and the family finally settled on Padmavathi from Chidambaram, daughter of the famous singer Sundaranar, and the wedding took place in September 1944 in the Self-Respect style of marriage propagated by the Dravidian movement – a wedding where garlands are exchanged by the bride and groom, without a thaali (mangalsutra), and especially without Brahmin priests officiating.

Karunanidhi appears to have fallen in love with his bride at first sight. In *Nenjukku Needhi*, he waxes eloquent about her qualities of patience, her love for him, her tolerance and her good-natured affection. He writes of wanting to earn a steady income for the first time in his life, as he wanted to protect and support his lovely wife.

To this end, the twenty-year-old struck a deal with the Dravida Nadigar Kazhagam (Dravidian Actors' Group) to write scripts for plays promoting the Dravidian ideology that would be staged across the state. The group had an additional request – that Karunanidhi must also act in the plays. He agreed, on the condition that he would only act in the plays that he himself scripted.

Karunanidhi and two of his friends who were also part of the troupe moved to Villupuram for a month to begin preparations for the play to be staged there. All three of them stayed in one room organized by the troupe manager. Karunanidhi describes those days of poverty in great detail.

> After finishing our morning ablutions, all of us would assemble at the venue of the drama. We would stand in line and sing a chorus – 'Dravidam Dravidam' was the song we sang instead of the traditional salute to the Gods. Then came a meagre breakfast. Once we ate, we would practise the play. It was after that that we could go and bathe.
>
> Bathing was a big problem there. Water was available only in some fields where farmers had installed taps. We had to walk far to find this, bathe quickly and wash our shirts and veshtis

> [dhotis] with some soap. During those times, the tears that would flow from my eyes and mingle with the water from the tap – only I knew about those.
>
> After bathing we would head home under the fierce sun. The smaller towel tied around our waists, the washed shirt thrown over one shoulder and the freshly cleaned veshti held over our heads as an umbrella, we would walk back. Once the clothes dried we would wear them and head for lunch. After consuming that 'punishment' we would rest for a while. Do you really think I would have been able to sleep?[16]

The play, titled *Palaniappan*, finally opened. It was a flop. The small audience that did come lauded it. But despite advertising, few people came. Periyar and Anna came to watch the play at different times. The collections were so poor that the owner of the troupe begged for Rs 10 from each of the leaders, who laughingly obliged him. The owner came up with the idea of renaming the play 'Santha', a woman's name, in an effort to draw crowds. That did not help either.

Karunanidhi explains what went wrong. In Villupuram in those days a vicious casteist mindset existed, he writes. He recounts conversations held in the streets there at that time.

> 'A drama company has come from Nagapattinam. There are over forty youngsters in that troupe. All of them are educated "parappasanga". They have named the company after "paraiyans" too.'
>
> 'Oh is that so? In that case their own caste fellows should only watch that drama.'

Paraiyar is the name of a scheduled caste in Tamil Nadu. Among the three major sub-castes amongst Dalits in the state – Pallars, Paraiyars and Arundhathiyars – the Paraiyars are predominantly spread across the northern and central belt of Tamil Nadu. The southern region is largely made up of the Pallar caste, while the western belt is home to the Arundhathiyars. Parappasanga, meaning Paraiyar boys, is often used as a derogatory term for Dalit Paraiyars in the state.

The word 'Dravida' in those days, writes Karunanidhi, was equated with the scheduled castes. Awareness about the ideology was yet to spread fully. The misconception about 'Dravida', he writes, was the cause for the drama to have flopped miserably.

Having wound up the play in Villupuram, Karunanidhi and the troupe proceeded to Pondicherry. In the little French colony, the play was a resounding success. People began referring to Karunanidhi as Sivaguru, the character he played in the drama.

A lawyer in the town sought out Karunanidhi and asked him to write an article for his magazine *Thozhilaalar Mithran* (Friend of the Labourers). Karunanidhi wrote a piece titled 'That Pen!' It was a critique of Gandhi and the Congress based on a pen that was lost from the Sabarmati Ashram.

Pondicherry's Congress workers were furious. A second article appeared – 'What if Gandhi Became the Viceroy?' A hunt began for Karunanidhi.

The opportunity came in the form of a public meeting organized in Pondicherry in which Periyar, Anna and Pattukottai Azhagirisamy participated. The meeting venue saw a sea of people. Among those were Congressmen shouting, 'Dravidian leaders! Go back!'

'"Come!" is the invitation that is the Tamilian's culture. What is the reason to say "Go"?' – these were the words with which Annadurai began his speech at the meeting. The Dravidar Kazhagam flag was hoisted at the end of the speeches. The minute the flag went up, Congressmen brought the pole down. Chaos descended along with the pole.

The leaders were whisked away by the Kazhagam cadre and hidden in the homes of supporters. Karunanidhi ran, chased by angry Congressmen. Separated from the crowd, he began to search in vain for a home that would offer him shelter. In desperation to escape from the mob, he entered a house outside which two women stood. They offered no objection. Congress workers barged into the house and dragged him out. One after the other, they beat him until he lost consciousness. Thinking that he was dead, they threw his unconscious body into the sewers and left. Two hours later Karunanidhi regained consciousness. An old lady and a young girl were looking upon him with great worry.

'Ayyo, whose child is this? He is lying as if dead,' exclaimed the old woman. She took him to her home, nursed him and helped him with a disguise, procuring a long kurta and skullcap, in order that he may be thought of as a Muslim. With this they called for a rickshaw and sent Karunanidhi on his way to where Periyar was staying.

Though it was late at night, Periyar and Anna had not slept, worrying about the fate of the young Karunanidhi. 'Are you okay?' asked the old man in a trembling voice. He then applied medicine with his own hands to Karunanidhi's wounds. 'Come with me, let us go,' said Periyar.[17]

Thus began his next journey – as an assistant editor with Periyar's *Kudiyarasu* magazine in Erode. For a year he worked and wrote for the magazine. From Coimbatore came a request – A.S.A. Saamy of Jupiter Films, a famous production house, sought Karunanidhi out to script films. He was to write the screenplay for the film *Rajakumari* to be produced by Jupiter Films.

'I told Periyar about the call. He said – "Carry on".'[18]

This would be the next turning point in Karunanidhi's life – his entry into the world of films and the first encounter with M.G. Ramachandran, a lifelong friend who would also turn foe.

In 1947, India attained Independence from nearly two centuries of British colonial rule. In 1948, Gandhi was shot dead by Nathuram Godse. Karunanidhi was facing his own loss. His beloved wife Padma, having birthed a male child, was on her deathbed. Though wracked with guilt and sorrow, Karunanidhi went on to address a public meeting in Pudukottai, putting ideology and cause above family.

By the time of his return, Padma had breathed her last. Karunanidhi writes of deep regret and a devastating sense of loss. 'Three years of married life – it seems she got bitter in that time! My teardrops fell on her stoic face and rolled down. Slowly I leaned towards her face. There were a number of women sitting around her. I did not bother about them. I kissed the forehead of my own woman. That was the only thing I had left to give her. She finished her chapter in my life in her twentieth year itself,' he writes.[19]

That same year, on 15 September, Karunanidhi's family fixed a second marriage for him. The infant M.K. Muthu needed a mother. A young girl from Thanjavur district was chosen. Dayalu was the daughter of Govindasamy, a middle-class farmer. Her elder brother Dakshinamoorthy was a Dravida ideologue and had even been imprisoned during protests.

On the day of the wedding, as Karunanidhi was awaiting the bride's entry, a group of student protesters marched by, shouting the slogans – 'Long live Periyar! Long live Tamil! Down with Hindi!' Karunanidhi, entranced, joined the protesters.

The young Dayalu had to wait for over an hour as relatives searched for the groom and finally found him near a school, shouting slogans along with the protesters. Karunanidhi, with this narrative, reveals yet again an intrinsic lack of interest in the banality of family life. 'Luckily, since I had habituated her (Dayalu) to wait for me on that first day itself, now no matter how late or how many days later I come home, she has learnt to tolerate it.'[20]

Dayalu, or Dayalu Ammal as she is respectfully referred to, would be the mother of four out of Karunanidhi's six children – Tamilarasu, Selvi, Alagiri and Stalin.

Karunanidhi would now climb the ladder within the Dravidar Kazhagam and, in the years to come, choose Annadurai as his mentor over Periyar and form a bridge between the two warring giants.

2

PERIYAR AND ANNADURAI

From the Justice Party to the Dravidar Kazhagam and Periyar's launching of the Self Respect and Social Justice Movement, better known as the Dravidian Movement, Tamil Nadu was charting its own course in history.

While large swathes of the country were enthralled by M.K. Gandhi, Jawaharlal Nehru, B.R. Ambedkar, Subhas Chandra Bose, Lal Bahadur Shastri and their ilk, leaders in Tamil Nadu opposed the Congress party and many of its resolutions. Their contribution to Indian history and politics has gone largely unrecorded.

Periyar, originally a Congressman who had joined the party in 1919, equally enamoured of Gandhi, broke away in 1925. The rift between him and other Congress leaders, most of whom were Brahmins, began in 1922. Until then, Periyar, a rich landlord, farmer and the owner of a rice mill, had given up his wealth to follow Gandhi's advocacy of austerity, spinning khadi and leading protests against the British.

In 1922, at the Tamil Nadu Congress Committee meeting held in Tirupur, Periyar wanted a resolution to be passed to end caste-based discrimination by allowing people of all castes to enter and worship in Hindu temples. The resolution was stalled. The staunch atheist who would mince no words swore that he would burn the Ramayana, the Manu Dharma Shastra as well as the Vedas to show his anger.

Periyar's resentment of Brahmins was a reflection of the anger already existing in the Madras Presidency of the time. Unlike in the northern states, where the Kshatriya and Vaishya castes had a robust population, in Tamil Nadu, the Kshatriyas and Vaishyas were almost absent. It was the Brahmins (the Shaivite Iyers and Vaishnavite Iyengars) followed by all other castes, which were classified as Sudras. Below them, outside of the Varnashrama Dharma, came the 'untouchables' or Dalits (Pallars, Paraiyars and Arundhathiyars), who were referred to by Gandhi as 'Harijans' or 'children of God'.

Communist intellectual Mythili Sivaraman documents the power wielded by the mere 3 per cent of Brahmins over all other castes in the Madras Presidency even as early as the 1800s:

> [W]hen the British found it expedient to offer English education to the Indians, it was the Brahmin with his exclusive tradition of learning that took the greatest advantage and filled the schools and colleges. Some of the non-Brahmins did follow suit later, pressurized by the growing impoverishment of villages, only to find that the Brahmin who formed only 3% of the population had established a virtual monopoly in all the fields of learning, administration and judiciary...
>
> More than anywhere else in India it was in Madras that the line between the Brahmin and the non-Brahmin was most sharply drawn. The social oppression of the 3% was of a content and

> scale unknown elsewhere. The Tamil Brahmin became symbolic of the worst kind of social segregation known to man. It was inevitable that the conflict between the Brahmin and the non-Brahmin communities long suppressed by religious sanctions should strive to find outlets.[1]

In 1924-25, Periyar would play a crucial role in the Vaikkom Satyagraha, a watershed event in the battle against untouchability. The Sri Mahadevar temple in Vaikkom, in the erstwhile Travancore area, now in Kerala, had since the 1800s been the cause for protests by the non-Brahmin Ezhava caste. They were not allowed to use the road leading to the temple or enter the temple itself. Kerala and Andhra Congress leaders led by Periyar conducted a satyagraha at the temple for months. Many were arrested and jailed.

People from all over the country began to pour in, demanding that untouchability be abolished. Periyar himself was jailed twice during the satyagraha. His wife Nagammai continued the protests in his absence. Finally, the temple roads were opened for all castes, although it was only in 1936 that the temple premises would be opened to all.

There is an oft-quoted saying by Periyar:

> Men should not touch each other, see each other; and cannot enter temples, fetch water from the village pond: in a land where such inhuman practices are ripe, it is a wonder that the earthquakes have not destroyed us, volcanoes not burnt us; it is a wonder that the earth has not split at its heart and plunged this land into an abyss; that a typhoon has not shattered us. I leave it to you to decide if you still like to trust a divinity that has not punished us thus; if you still consider that God a just God, a Merciful Being. How long do you desire a vast section of the

> oppressed, the depressed classes to remain patient, peaceful and quiet? Would you consider it wrong if these oppressed were to choose death rather than lead such a life as they do now?

Periyar, or The Elder, whose given name was E.V. Ramasamy Naicker, believed that the Varnaashrama Dharma, or the caste system, was the root of many evils in society. He was also an atheist and rationalist – he believed that any religion was only meant to subdue and suppress the downtrodden. By 1925, angered by what he saw as Gandhi's support of the caste system, he decided to leave the party for good.

The straw that broke the camel's back was a school called Gurukulam in Kallidaikurichi village run by V.V.S. Iyer, a Congress leader. 'A fierce controversy raged through the Congress when it was discovered that non-Brahmins in this school had to eat away from the Brahmins. In this atmosphere of intense acrimony Periyar walked out of the Provincial Congress Committee meet in Kanchipuram and left the Congress for good a little later. His entire political outlook and career took a violent turnaround.'[2]

In a searing editorial in his magazine *Kudiyarasu* on 29 March 1931, Periyar wrote at length in criticism of Gandhi: 'The day when Gandhi said God alone guides him, that Varnashrama Dharma is a superior system fit to govern the affairs of the world and that everything happens according to God's will, we came to the conclusion that there is no difference between Gandhism and Brahminism. We also concluded that unless the Congress party that subscribes to such philosophy and principle is abolished it will not be good for the country. But now this fact has been found out at least by some of the people. They have gained wisdom and courage to call for the downfall of Gandhism. This is a great victory to our cause.'

The break with Gandhi and the Congress, the formation and coming to power of the Justice Party and the launch of the Self Respect Movement all took place in the early- to mid-1920s. Periyar gravitated to the Justice Party, the only real opposition to the Congress at the time, which was a group of elite non-Brahmins and espoused their cause. The Congress's wave of popularity had overtaken the Justice Party, which found itself flailing and thrashing for life. Periyar was the man of the masses, speaking their language – direct, voluble, harsh and unflinching in his anger and diatribe against the Brahmin. He became the leader of the Justice Party and renamed it as the Dravidar Kazhagam.

The rise of leaders such as Pattukottai Azhagirisamy, the poet Bharatidasan, Maraimalai Adigal, Thiru Vi Kalyanasundaranar as well as the young C.N. Annadurai followed.

An intense social reform movement was launched by Periyar against the caste system and untouchability. With the clarion call of atheism, he famously stated:

> There is no god
> There is no god at all
> He who invented god is a fool
> He who propagates god is a knave
> He who worships god is a barbarian.

He and his followers barged into temples along with the 'untouchables', garlanding idols with chappals or smashing them in a dramatic effort to drive home the message that religion and caste are the root of discrimination in society. The reins of power in society and in government at the time were in the hands of the educated Brahmins, while the majority of the other castes were denied education and basic standards of living. What Periyar and his followers did was to bring to the fore a 'non-Brahmin' consciousness of sorts, banding the majority together in revolt against the so-called 'upper caste'. The coinage of terms such as 'suyamariyadhai' (self-respect) helped catapult the movement into a popular rebellion.

What they did not, however, do was to ensure the unshackling of the 'untouchables' – this was done rather more successfully in pockets by the communist parties. As Sivaraman writes in her candid dissection of the Dravidian movement and Periyar's role in the 1971 issue of her magazine *The Radical Review*, the 'untouchable' Dalits were left out of the Dravidian movement, which only managed to move non-Brahmins into the seats of power occupied earlier by the Brahmins:

> Centred in the non-Brahmin lower castes, Periyar's movement concerned the Harijans only marginally. Apart from the Vaikkom struggle of the 1920s, Periyar never took up any of the major causes of the Harijans. In fact, his use of the term 'non-Brahmin' precludes them. They are addressed as the depressed classes. They are not even described as Tamilians, but as Adi-Dravidas.
>
> Periyar's attitude to them has been, at best, paternalistic... With increasing urbanization and the spread of literacy, it was inevitable that Brahmin hegemony should crumble and non-Brahmins move into erstwhile Brahmin preserves.

In 1937, the first wave of anti-Hindi protests broke out in Madras Presidency as then Chief Minister Rajagopalachari introduced a law to make the learning of Hindi compulsory in schools. Over the next three decades, the Self Respect Movement and the Dravidar Kazhagam would grow larger and larger, turning into a massive revolution that the Congress simply could not handle.

DIFFERENCES ARISE

As the revolution progressed, so did the acrimony between its leaders increase. The first open break between two key leaders came in 1947, when Periyar announced that 15 August, the momentous day of Indian Independence, was to be a day of mourning. His logic was that the country was going from the hands of the relatively unbiased British into those of the 'upper castes' who had taken over the Indian National Congress.

Annadurai disagreed openly with his mentor Periyar. 'It is not a sad day, 15 August is a joyous day,' he stated. 'It is incorrect to view through the narrow lens of our ideology such a momentous occasion watched by the world. 15 August is a day that will herald the end of two hundred years of suppression and rancour; it is an important day for Dravidam too,' he said.[3]

This caused a deep rift within the Dravidar Kazhagam. At a subsequent public meeting held in Tuticorin, Anna was absent while Periyar attended. The bitterness between the two leaders appeared to be increasing. Pattukottai Azhagirisamy, firmly on Periyar's side, would continually criticize Anna in harsh terms. Karunanidhi wrote an editorial in *Murasoli* in sharp criticism of those opportunists who were attempting to widen the rift between Periyar and Anna. Angered Dravidar Kazhagam workers stopped his next edition from being printed.

Eventually, the rancour eased and, on 23 and 24 October 1948, Periyar organized a large public meeting of the Dravidar Kazhagam in his hometown Erode in demand of a separate Dravida state. The chief guest at the function was Annadurai. 'I have given the keys to the box in Anna's hand,'[4] said the elderly man, signalling a shift in the leadership of the movement and the Kazhagam.

Did Karunanidhi realize then that his star had to be hitched to Annadurai's wagon, as he was the heir apparent to the movement and the Kazhagam? One cannot be sure as only Karunanidhi can confirm that. What is certain is that the brilliant protégé did in fact ensure that he protected and defended his chosen mentor in public, even at the cost of earning the ire of the elders of the movement.

Take, for instance, the anecdote narrated vividly by Karunanidhi himself in *Nenjukku Needhi*. Anjaa Nenjan Pattukottai Azhagirisamy's health was failing rapidly. At the Erode conference, he announced that it would be his last rally as his illness was winning over his will.

Karunanidhi recounts how Anna resolved to help Azhagirisamy at any cost and took him to a hospital in Tambaram, Chennai, in a bid to cure him. Anna announced that whosoever invited him to speak at a public meeting would have to send Rs 100 first to Azhagirisamy's family and only upon getting a receipt for the same would he oblige. Still, the doctors at Tambaram were unable to save Azhagirisamy and suggested that he return home.

At the railway station, as Azhagirisamy was carried on a stretcher into the train, 'his eyes turned into lakes'. He beckoned Mathiyazhagan, a friend standing nearby, and said to him, 'Tell Anna, Azhagiri has finally understood who his friends and who his foes are,' sobbed the old man.[5] Anna wiped his tears away as he walked out of the station. What Azhagiri meant was that despite him having been a staunch supporter of Periyar and a harsh open critic of Anna, it was the latter who had risen to the occasion and helped him in his hour of need.

Azhagirisamy died shortly afterward in Thanjavur in 1949. Thousands of admirers arrived in the beautiful town to accompany the Anjaa Nenjan on his last journey. Anna and his followers organized a massive cultural festival in honour of the late leader. Through this, they managed to collect Rs 6,000, a princely sum for that time. This money was handed over to the poverty-ridden family of Azhagirisamy.

What Karunanidhi did next was characteristic. At a students' meeting organized in Thanjavur itself, he criticized Periyar for not having cared for Azhagiri in his last days. His friend Anbazhagan, the current general secretary of the DMK, also spoke along the same lines.

When Periyar heard of this, he issued a statement that no one should invite Karunanidhi or Anbazhagan to any event or meeting. He also wrote that it was at Anna's bidding that both had spoken out against him. 'I was shocked at Periyar's statement. But I did not give him a response,' wrote Karunanidhi in his autobiography.[6]

In 1949, Periyar and Rajaji, sworn political enemies who remained lifelong friends, had a secret meeting in Tiruvannamalai. Rajaji was then the Governor General of India. Despite being asked a number of times, Periyar refused to divulge what had transpired between the two. On 19 June 1949, he finally published a statement in his magazine *Viduthalai* (freedom). His discussion with Rajaji had been about creating an heir for himself, he said; that he was no longer able to travel and work as before; and that he was unable to see anyone who could take over that responsibility.

Nine days later, on 28 June 1949, he published a statement again in *Viduthalai*. 'It is necessary and urgent for me to create a legal heir for myself and for my wealth and property. To this end, I have decided to hand it over to Maniammai, whom I have known for the past five or six years and who has gained my trust, who has concern for my well-being and for the well-being of the movement. Along with her, four or five people will be chosen to run a trust for party funds, for which the papers are being prepared. In order to ensure that it is legally sound, if there are some words used that are to the distaste of many, let no one fear that the ideology or the movement will disintegrate,' he wrote.[7]

The cat was out of the bag. Seventy-two-year-old Periyar wanted to marry twenty-six-year-old K.A. Maniammai, his personal assistant of about five years. Stating that this move was against the ideological foundation of the movement, many party leaders and cadre wrote to Periyar, impressing upon him not to go ahead with the marriage. On 9 July 1949, Periyar and Maniammai were married. Unaware of this, the Dravidar Kazhagam Administrative Committee under the leadership of Anna met on 10 July and passed a resolution requesting Periyar not to go ahead with the wedding. That same day, a letter arrived stating that the marriage ceremony was complete.

Periyar's move had left many leaders frothing in fury – not because he had married a much younger woman, but because he had announced her as his heir and handed over the party funds to her. Many leaders had dedicated their lives to Periyar's movement and they felt cheated.

Anna began to collect the names of the Kazhagam cadre who had resigned and published them in his own paper, *Dravida Nadu,* under a column titled 'Kanneer Thuligal' (teardrops).

Anna announced that in Madras's Pavalakaara Street, on 17 September 1949, also Periyar's birthday, a meeting of the Dravidar Kazhagam would take place under the aegis of K.K. Neelamegam, a leader who had fallen out with Periyar. At this meeting, poet Bharatidasan made a speech demanding that Periyar be removed forthwith from the Kazhagam.

Annadurai, however, differed. He said at the meeting that removing Periyar and taking over the Kazhagam would be akin to climbing a tree to pluck fruit with a black cobra wound around a leg. It was at this meeting that Anna first mooted the idea of starting afresh – a new political party by the name of Dravida

Munnetra Kazhagam (DMK) with the same ideals and ideology as practised and propounded by Periyar.

That same evening, a celebration was held at Royapuram's Robinson Park in Madras to launch the DMK. At that launch, Anna spoke with fervour: 'Most importantly, the very first duty to be done is to oppose any government which attempts to suppress freedom to write, freedom of speech. In this, the Dravida Munnetra Kazhagam must be at the forefront and fight like an army. Come!' he exhorted.[8]

THE SECOND WAVE OF ANTI-HINDI PROTESTS

On 2 May 1950, Congress minister Madhava Menon announced that Hindi would be a compulsory language from standards 1 to 6 in all schools. A massive agitation began once again and this time it was larger than the first one. The DMK, with over 50,000 members and 700 branches, had turned into an army. Led by Anna, anti-Hindi protests rocked the state. Jails were filled and DMK cadre were beaten by the police. Such was the pressure that within two months of the rule, Menon was forced to modify his statement: Hindi was now not compulsory but only a voluntary subject.[9]

Protests, though, continued – in railway stations, against the use of Hindi on trains and in front of shops owned by north Indians. DMK and DK men applied tar over the Hindi words written on trains in an attempt to show their opposition. In Trichy, Periyar and Karunanidhi together blacked out the Hindi names on the trains and the station. As the DMK marched behind Karunanidhi, shouting slogans, a car pulled up next to them and Periyar warmly wished Karunanidhi. 'Despite having parted ways with bitterness into two parties, this sudden encounter showed me that the affection and love had not diminished in the least,' writes Karunanidhi.[10]

The DMK under Anna, and the DK under Periyar, protested for the same cause but separately. Periyar won many victories in this time. He got caste names removed from railway canteens and from establishments across the state.

BUILDING A PARTY

'On 15 September 1949, when it was raining, clouds were thundering, people were with empty purses and the press was discordant, we started the Dravida Munnetra Kazhagam. I always remember that it was a rainy day when the DMK came into existence. Today, people consider that we are the biggest political storm that they have to face,'[11] said C.N. Annadurai, founder of the party that would bend the Congress juggernaut to its will.

In a state where the Congress and the communists had strong support, the fledgling DMK worked with joy and abandon to create a new political alternative. Youngsters flocked to the party from the nooks and corners of Tamil Nadu. Annadurai, Nedunchezhian, Karunanidhi and others worked tirelessly to build the party from the bottom up.

There were troubles galore. Congressmen came into the DMK fold, seeing in the young party an opportunity to further their careers in a loaded political climate. Factions arose and, with them, differences.

Karunanidhi gives one instance of how he helped to resolve a problem between warring factions in Trichy, the heart of Tamil Nadu. This is a telling example of the bond he built with the party cadre at the grassroots level from the very beginning, something he maintained until he could no longer be active in politics.

Around the time of the second wave of the anti-Hindi protests, Annadurai was fuming. The Trichy branch of the DMK was simply not working or expanding, thanks to internecine conflict. Anna issued an ultimatum: that he would not go to Trichy to address any public meeting until the issue was amicably resolved.

Karunanidhi, Ponmalai Parangusam, Anbil Dharmalingam and a few others, worried at the turn of events, approached Anna to plead with him to change his mind. But Anna stood firm. 'Due to the inner party conflicts in Trichy, the Kazhagam itself is getting destroyed. Until you rectify it and show me, I will not speak at any meeting in Trichy,' he said.

'But it is only if you come and speak will things get better, Anna,' said Parangusam.

'First conduct meetings there with Karunanidhi. If there is life left in the party there, I will come,' retorted Anna.[12]

The team of young DMK leaders rushed to Trichy. Karunanidhi addressed the local cadre in a meeting. 'If you show that you are building the Kazhagam and nurturing it, then this will in itself bring Anna here,' said Karunanidhi. A pep talk followed and the cadre rose as one. 'Long live Anna,' echoed in Trichy as enthusiastic DMK workers began preparing for meetings across the district. This was the first time 'flag-hoisting functions' were organized. Taking the cue from Trichy, other district cadre of the DMK began inviting Karunanidhi to do the same all over the state – requests that Karunanidhi happily obliged.

A year later, the Trichy branch was working as one and making rapid progress. Old handloom clothes had to be sold to collect funds for the party. As it was being discussed as to who would sell them in Trichy, Annadurai piped up: 'I will sell it there.'[13]

The very same Trichy which had witnessed so much conflict was now the venue chosen by Annadurai in 1956 to hold a massive meeting. A crucial decision was taken by the cadre of the DMK in this meeting: to enter electoral politics, a key departure from Periyar's stand.

In 1951 was held the very first state meeting of the DMK. Independent India was going into polls for the first time as a free nation in 1952. From the morning of 17 November 1951 until the morning of 18 November non-stop, the DMK's General Body debated over whether or not to enter the electoral fray.

It was finally resolved that the DMK would not contest in 1952: 'Without getting the views of the Dravidians, without concern for the lives of Dravidians, the Indian laws have been written in an authoritarian manner by one party. This is condemned by the DMK and, as a result, the Kazhagam will not contest the 1952 election...The DMK will support any candidate not belonging to the Congress or the Communists who has a progressive, intelligent bent of mind,' read the resolution.[14]

The DMK then went on to fiercely oppose many moves by the Rajaji-led Congress government in Tamil Nadu. In 1953, it was the 'Modified Scheme of Elementary Education', wherein students would go to school for half a day and, for the rest, learn the profession of their parents. This scheme the DMK and the DK condemned and agitated against as being casteist and propagating caste. Another set of protests broke out demanding that the name of a small town called Dalmiyapuram be changed to Kallakudi, its Tamil name.

The day 15 June 1953 would put on display another classic Karunanidhi gimmick. The 'Kallakudi' protest, hailed by staunch DMK men as a legendary demonstration by their 'Kalaignar', would take place on that day.

Around 10 a.m., when DMK members led by Karunanidhi were protesting at the Dalmiyapuram railway station, having pasted the Tamil name Kallakudi on the boards of the station, a train chugged in. Karunanidhi and four others lay down on the track in front of the train in protest in a symbolic gesture and were detained by the police. Other DMK men continued this over the next few hours until a lathi-charge resulted.

Karunanidhi, who was never in any real danger of the train running over him, was eventually hailed as 'Kallakudi Veerar', or Kallakudi Hero. He was sentenced to two months in jail and a fine of Rs 35. He chose not to pay the fine and spent an additional month in jail. The protests demanding the name change to Kallakudi continued for another 100 days.

THE FIRST ELECTION

From 17 to 20 May 1956 was held the second state conference of the DMK at Trichy. All members of the DMK were called upon to vote on whether or not the party should jump into the electoral fray and prop up candidates in the next election to be held in 1957. Two boxes were kept at the venue – the red box was for those in favour of entering electoral politics and the black for those who did not think it was a wise move. Into the red box were cast 56,942 votes, while 4,203 votes went into the black one.

In 1957, the DMK entered the poll fray. Karunanidhi contested from the Kulithalai seat in Karur district. He won his first assembly seat. The party, which although did not topple the Congress, managed to win fifteen assembly and two parliamentary seats in its very first election, with a total of 17 lakh votes. Annadurai sat in the seat of the leader of the opposition.

In 1959, the DMK emerged as the single largest party in the elections to the Madras municipal corporation, with forty-five seats. A.P. Arasu became the DMK's first mayor of Madras.[15]

From 1963 onwards, the DMK would lead the anti-Hindi agitations across the state. Students and youngsters, mesmerized by the cause, joined the agitations in droves. Rioting and violence were the norm over the next five years. If in 1963 it was about pressuring Prime Minister Nehru to stop the move of announcing Hindi as the official language, by 1965, as the date of enactment of the Official Languages Act loomed closer, large-scale rioting broke out – first in Madurai and then across the state. Two police officers were killed in the violence and around seventy died as college students jumped into the agitation. Arson, looting, lathi-charges and firing were commonplace during this time as normal life came to a standstill. The Congress government called in paramilitary forces and Prime Minister Lal Bahadur Shastri had to backtrack on declaring Hindi as the official language of the country, keeping English, instead, as the official language for an indefinite period of time.

The fierce protests showed the DMK's might and popularity. In the 1967 elections, the DMK came to power for the first time. N. Ram, chairman and publisher of the *Hindu* group of newspapers, was a young journalist at the time, watching history unfold before his eyes. 'We did not realize then that 1967 would herald a change. It would be a watershed moment for Tamil Nadu,' he says.

With 138 seats, on 6 March 1967, Annadurai took oath as the first DMK Chief Minister of Tamil Nadu. Karunanidhi was sworn in as the minister for public works, housing, highways, transport and ports. The Congress would never come back to power in the state.

3

RISE TO POWER

The first blot on the new DMK government would come from the remote village of Keezhvenmani in the rich rice bowl of Thanjavur district. On 25 December 1968, a mob of rich 'upper caste' landlords descended upon the Dalit agricultural labourers of Keezhvenmani in the dead of night, torching their homes and burning alive forty-four men, women and children.

'Huts without roof. Huts without walls. Huts ground to dust. To ash. Huts with broken bangle pieces. A silence that ill became a *cheri* (a Harijan street) accustomed to barking dogs, screeching children, gossiping women and drunken brawls.'[1] These are the words of Communist Party of India (Marxist) member and journalist Mythili Sivaraman, whose searing accounts of the Keezhvenmani horror in the *Economic and Political Weekly* brought the issue to the fore.

The issue was one of caste, a resurgent Dalit population and an enraged Mirasdar (landowner) minority that took the law into its own hands and even got away with cold-blooded murder. The

DMK government – much later – bore the brunt of criticism for not doing enough to prevent the massacre.

As Sivaraman details in her work, tensions had been building for over three months prior to the incident in Keezhvenmani village. The reason for this was the skewed land ownership pattern that was the norm in Tamil Nadu at the time. 'Of all the districts in Tamil Nadu, Thanjavur has the most skewed land ownership pattern. In 1961, 3.8 per cent of the cultivating households, owning more than 15 acres of land each, held 25.88 per cent of the cultivated area while 76 per cent, owning up to 5 acres each, held only 37 per cent of the area. Thanjavur also has the highest proportion of landless labourers: for every 10 cultivators, there were 9 labourers in 1961. The 1971 Census found 41 per cent of the rural population to be landless labour while the state average was 29 per cent. Thanjavur also has the highest percentage of Harijans amongst the landless. A combination of these factors had made Thanjavur a classic setting for feudal oppression.'[2]

Since late 1967 itself, Dalit agricultural labourers had been organized by the communists into the Agricultural Workers' Union. The labourers of Keezhvenmani demanded higher wages in a year (1966) when paddy produce was low. They wanted 'half a litre more' of rice.[3] Enraged 'upper caste' zamindars refused. They in turn formed a Paddy Producers' Association (PPA) and began to bring in labourers from outside the district, from areas such as Nagapattinam. Keezhvenmani's labourers did not allow the outsiders to work. Clashes ensued and, as Sivaraman documents, three workers of the CPM were killed in the three months leading up to the fatal night of 25 December.

In November 1968, the district secretary of the CPM-led Agricultural Workers' Union, P. Ramamurthy, wrote an urgent letter to the chief secretary of the Annadurai-led government, asking for protection, as even the police were biased. Sivaraman writes of the irony of how the chief minister spoke at a public meeting of 'what threat there could be in his regime to the lives of "Ramamurthy's partymen"?'

Subsequent eyewitness accounts revealed the horror of that night: landlords surrounding the Dalit colony from three directions, cutting off escape routes and setting huts on fire. Women and children who took refuge in a hut were locked in and set aflame. Some women threw babies out of the burning huts in a desperate attempt to save their children. The landlords and their men threw these babies back inside the flames.[4]

Two court cases were initiated: one against twenty-two Dalit labourers of Keezhvenmani for the murder of a landlord's agent, Pakkirisami, and the second against twenty-three landlords for the murder of forty-two (the state government's official death count, although the Centre later said it was forty-four) Dalit men, women and children.

In the first case, the Nagapattinam sessions court convicted eight people, one for life. In the second case too, eight people were convicted to ten years of rigorous imprisonment each. When the cases went on appeal, the high court upheld the judgement in the first case while acquitting the landlords in the second.

Sivaraman wrote:

> ...there was something astonishing about the fact that all of the 23 persons implicated in the case should be mirasdars [landowners]. Most of them were rich men, owning vast extent of lands, and Gopala Krishna Naidu [key accused and president of the PPA] possessed a car. However much they might have been eager to wreak vengeance on the kisans, it was difficult to believe that they would walk bodily to the scene and set fire to the houses, unaided by any of their servants. They were more

> likely to play safe, unlike desperate, hungry labourers. One would rather expect that the mirasdars, keeping themselves in the background, would send their servants to commit the several offences which according to the prosecution the mirasdars personally committed...The evidence did not enable Their Lordships to identify and punish the guilty.

'In brief, gentlemen farmers will also be gentlemen killers,'[5] she wrote.

This was the first acid test of the fledgling DMK government under the larger-than-life Annadurai. The chief minister rushed two of his ministers, Karunanidhi and Law Minister Madhavan, to Keezhvenmani. The government failed in this first big test. Little action was taken and the prosecution did a shoddy job in court, allowing the landlords, whose leader Gopala Krishna Naidu was a known supporter of the Congress party, to get away scot-free. Justice, however, caught up with Naidu in the form of a youth called Nandan, who led a gang that hacked Naidu in 1980. Nandan was said to be an eyewitness to the Keezhvenmani carnage.[6]

On 27 January 1969, communist MLA B. Jayaraj moved a motion in the legislative assembly: 'This House censures and disapproves of the policy of the ministry in particular respect, namely, its failure to maintain law and order in Thanjavur district, resulting in the ghastly incident of arson on 25 December 1968 in the village of Kilvenmani and the death of forty-two innocent women, children and old men.'[7]

But, by this time, cancer was eating away Anna's body. It would overpower him on 3 February 1969. 'Before the Keezhvenmani motion was taken up for discussion in the assembly, a new ministry headed by M. Karunanidhi was formed consequent on the demise of Chief Minister Late Dr C.N. Annadurai. The motion thus became infructuous,' show the records of House proceedings.[8]

FAREWELL ANNA, VANAKKAM KARUNA

Thousands turned out on the streets of Madras to bid Annadurai farewell as he was laid to rest at a memorial on Marina Beach.

Karunanidhi, by this time, had gathered support for himself amongst the key younger leaders of the party. The next in line to Anna was 'Naavalar' (poet) C.R. Nedunchezhian, a towering figure of the DMK, who, along with Anna, was a founder member of the party.

As early as 1959, Karunanidhi, according to old-timers in the party as well as senior journalists in the state, had successfully manipulated Annadurai into making a public display of his affection for Karunanidhi, in the process indicating that he was next in line as leader of the party.

Karunanidhi himself writes of this episode at a meeting of DMK cadre held on 15 April 1959 at Marina Beach, following a huge victory in the local body polls that year. In *Nenjukku Needhi*, Karunanidhi recollects Anna's words:

> People have told me that only Karunanidhi can lead us to victory in this election. I said it is not possible. My words were hasty. I regret them now. 'If we win, what will you give me?' Karunanidhi had asked. Under the impression that I wouldn't have to give anything, I had said I will give him a one 'poun' gold ring. I have never gone to a jewellery shop to buy anything even for my wife. But since these forty-five young rogues have managed to snatch a huge victory, I went to the store myself and bought a ring for this young bull [Karunanidhi]...This ring is not the fruit of his efforts. It symbolizes the enormous affection and love that Karunanidhi has in my heart.[9]

Senior journalists in the state, though, recount that Karunanidhi had in fact played a trick on Anna. They say that Karunanidhi had himself bought the ring and privately requested Anna to appreciate him in front of the cadre. This, they say, is characteristic of how keen a politician Karunanidhi was and how he systematically sidelined any opposition to his ascension as leader of the DMK.

Perhaps the incident of the ring sat firmly in the minds of the DMK cadre. Perhaps their frequent interactions with Karunanidhi during election campaigns had endeared him to them. Perhaps his oratorical skills and youthful energy had impressed them. Or perhaps it was a combination of all of these – but when Annadurai died, Karunanidhi suddenly had a large number of supporters rooting for him, much to the chagrin of Nedunchezhiyan, the seniormost leader after Anna and a minister in his cabinet.

While his opponents and critics describe him as ruthless when it came to the pursuit of power, Karunanidhi predictably gives it a softer spin in his autobiography.

The first MLA who came to Karunanidhi's support in the wake of Anna's death was Modakurichi legislator Erode Chinnasamy. Ministers Mathiyazhagan, Sathyavani Muthu, A. Govindasamy, Sadiq Batcha and other MLAs arrived at Karunanidhi's residence and a clamour began for him to take over as chief minister. 'For me, who had been opining that Naavalar [Nedunchezhiyan] should be the next chief minister, this sudden turn of events was painful,' he writes.[10]

'When we all discussed who should become the chief minister, the majority of the voices said Kalaignar. I too have been insisting that you take up that responsibility. Despite all of this, he has not agreed. He sent Maran to tell us that Kalaignar does not want to become chief minister and not to disturb him. We told him this was for the party and for the people,' M.G. Ramachandran, cine star and a member of the DMK, later said at a public meeting of the party in April 1969.[11]

Karunanidhi, in his book, is at pains to portray himself as one who did not covet the chief minister's chair. He writes about resigning himself to the pressures from the party and going to meet Nedunchezhiyan to discuss the turn of events. Karunanidhi quotes a bitter Nedunchezhiyan as stating: 'I will be chief minister. If not, I will not take up any ministership.'[12] Karunanidhi continues to describe how he pleaded with the leader to become a minister as well as the leader of the legislative party in the assembly. Nedunchezhiyan was resolute in his refusal.

On 10 February 1969, Karunanidhi became chief minister for the first time. Periyar, Rajaji, Finance Minister Morarji Desai, former Chief Minister Bhaktavatsalam and others wished the young man warmly.

Upcountry newspapers, however, were not that kind. Karunanidhi, in *Nenjukku Needhi,* writes of stinging reports and editorials written by dailies such as *The Mail, Amrita Bazaar Patrika* and others describing him as a 'terrorist' for having led many strong protests against the imposition of Hindi.

Rumblings began within the party, with senior leader Nedunchezhiyan wounded and obstinate in his refusal to climb down. Karunanidhi felt the desperate need to keep the party together in this challenging time. His other mentor, Periyar, who also realized the crucial need for the DMK to stick together, stepped in to help.

On 11 February 1969, in his magazine *Viduthalai,* Periyar wrote a frank and open letter of advice to Nedunchezhiyan and the cadre of the DMK. 'In this situation, what should not have happened, although it did, is Naavalar's discontent. If this discontent increases, it will have bad results and enmity. The chief minister's post does not belong to Kalaignar or to Naavalar.

This is the wealth of the Tamils. Naavalar and Kalaignar are only trustees. I request both of them to understand this. I believe that no one should look upon this [post] with a sense of right or ego. In public life, looking upon something as a right or with ego amounts to selfishness.'[13]

In subsequent open letters in *Viduthalai*, Periyar continued to praise Karunanidhi and announced his complete faith in the young man, while calling upon Nedunchezhiyan to relent. Finally, Naavalar buckled. On 13 August 1969, V.R. Nedunchezhiyan became the minister for education and health and also the leader of the House with his younger colleague Karunanidhi as chief minister.

THE 1970S

In his brief stint as chief minister, Annadurai had passed some key legislation, including the change of name of the state to Tamil Nadu from Madras Province, and also introduced legislation to scrap the three-language formula and have a two-language one instead – effectively throwing Hindi out of the state. Abiding by the ideals of the Dravidian movement that he was associated with for so many decades, Anna also made legal the Self Respect Marriage, ceremonies that did not have Brahmin priests officiating and which did not need the thaali or mangalsutra. This act was called the Hindu Marriage (Madras Amendment) Act 1967, and Tamil Nadu is the only state in the country to allow such a marriage.

The most important move that Anna carried out was also a poll promise on the eve of the 1967 elections – three 'measures' of rice for a rupee. This was a continuation of the social welfare policies begun by his predecessor Kamaraj of the Congress party.

During Anna's tenure, Karunanidhi held the transport portfolio as well. It was during this period that he nationalized transport corporations, paving the way for cheaper and more effective connections within the state.

'It was similar to Indira Gandhi's move of nationalizing banks,' says author and scholar V. Geetha. 'Many people mocked him saying it [nationalizing transport] was done to make it easier for people to go watch films but I don't agree with that. The reality is that this move achieved excellent connectivity in Tamil Nadu and led to growth.'

Once in the chief minister's chair from February 1969, Karunanidhi actively got involved in governance and in speeding up reforms. The first scheme announced by his government was the 'Manu Neethi Thittam' – justice for petitions. Under this scheme, government officials went to the people directly, collected petitions and resolved their issues on the spot. This scheme was introduced on 15 September 1969. From then till 30 September 1974, 8.35 lakh petitions were received. Of these, 7.7 lakh were redressed, a success rate of 92.2 per cent.[14] This scheme also set the bureaucracy of the state on the path of being in constant touch with the people and bringing in a culture of accessibility into the Tamil Nadu government.

In 1970, the DMK shifted focus to a crucial issue that propagated inequity in society: land ownership. The Tamil Nadu Land Reform (Fixation of Ceiling on Land) Act of 1961 was amended by Karunanidhi to cap land ownership at a maximum of 15 acres. Surplus lands were then redistributed to the poor, landless farmers and the scheduled castes and scheduled tribes. According to government records, 1.79 lakh acres were taken over after the act was passed, and distributed to 1.37 lakh landless poor farmers, of whom close to 62,000 were Dalits and 204 scheduled tribes. In 1971 was enacted the Conferment of Ownership Act, which ensured that farmers became the owners of the residential plot they lived on. Rights of ownership were also granted to tenant farmers who tilled the soil, rather than the rich zamindars in whose name the patta was held.

There are criticisms of this reform too. Based on the data available for the period up to 1999, Dr M. Thangaraj of the Madras Institute of Development Studies encapsulates what went wrong with the well-intentioned reforms as they were implemented across the state:

> Significantly, the guidelines for the distribution of the ceiling-surplus land show that preference will be given to agricultural labourers belonging to the Scheduled Castes and Scheduled Tribes. But the data on distribution of ceiling-surplus land shows that 61 per cent of the land was distributed to others (non-Scheduled Castes and non-Scheduled Tribes). It is clear that the implementing officers have vested interest and hence the benefit of ceiling-surplus land could not fully reach the target groups.[15]

One of the major reasons why the land ceiling act failed to acquire more land for distribution is the advance public announcement about the proposed act. The announcement, say experts, gave enough time for many big landlords to circumvent the law through fictitious transfers of land. According to one estimate, an extent of 31,970.16 ha (79,000 acres) had been transferred a few weeks before the Ceiling on Land Holdings Act came into force.

Another reason attributed to its failure is the exemption it granted to public trusts. 'There had been hectic transfer of hundreds of acres to trusts. Thanjavur district has scores of public trusts possessing thousands of acres. The higher level of ceiling and also the allowances made for a family of more than five members also significantly reduced the extent of surplus land,' says S. Viswanathan in an article in *Frontline* magazine.[16]

By 1972, tensions were brewing within the party left behind by Annadurai. This time, though, it was not Nedunchezhiyan but a friend of Karunanidhi's who finally broke the camel's back. M.G. Ramachandran, a much loved cine star who was brought into politics and the DMK by Karunanidhi, rebelled. MGR, it is said, wanted the post of health minister. Karunanidhi, perhaps well aware of MGR's popularity amongst the masses, declined. A furious MGR made his move. As party treasurer at the time, MGR openly accused Karunanidhi of siphoning off party funds. Karunanidhi expelled him from the DMK. MGR took with him fewer than a dozen legislators and about half the cadre of the party and formed his Anna Dravida Munnetra Kazhagam (ADMK). But more on MGR later.

In 1969, as Karunanidhi took over as chief minister of the state, Prime Minister Indira Gandhi in Delhi too was facing troubles of her own. She was on the warpath with senior Congress leaders over a number of issues. Gandhi supported independent candidate V.V. Giri over the Congress party's choice of S. Nijalingappa for the post of President of India. She also went ahead with the nationalization of banks without consulting Finance Minister Morarji Desai. All of this culminated in the Congress president expelling her from the party. The grand old party split into two: the Indira-led Congress (R) – R for Requisition – and the Nijalingappa- and Kamaraj-led Congress (O) – O for Organization.

Most Congress members of Parliament went over to Gandhi's side. But to sail through, she needed crucial support from smaller parties. Karunanidhi, quick to smell an opportunity, offered his support to Gandhi – with a rider: the Lok Sabha seats would be fought by the Congress in the alliance, while the assembly seats would go to the DMK. In this manner, with his extraordinary ability to bargain and arm-twist, Karunanidhi, for the first time in the history of the DMK, forged an alliance with a party that it had thus far fought and railed against.

The 1970s were also about severe police repression and a ruthless crackdown on striking trade unions. The DMK government under Karunanidhi broke the back of the labour movement and, in its wake, that of the communists, who had pockets of support across the state.

CPM leader Mythili Sivaraman is perhaps one of the best chroniclers of the repression of the time, as she travelled widely across the state to tiny villages and also participated in agitations against industry units as a member of the party. She writes in the January 1970 issue of her magazine, *The Radical Review*, of Karunanidhi: 'The present Chief Minister has warned trade unions not to put forward "unreasonable demands" and has made it plain that "the government would not hesitate to take firm action to curb violence indulged in by workers with a view to forcing managements to concede their demands".'

She goes on to quote the chief minister: 'When conditions of labour in many of the industries in India were generally much better and the amenities given much larger and more elaborate than in some of the developing countries, the agitational approach to all problems, more often on issues unrelated to trade union activities, caused only annoyance, stagnation and loss in production.'[17]

The DMK government, since it came to power in 1967 under Annadurai and subsequently led by Karunanidhi from 1969, embarked on a systematic process of creating its own trade unions, thereby splintering the unity of labourers and workers in industry. Sivaraman writes about how the DMK union brokered a reluctant peace in a new Britannia factory at Ambattur on the outskirts of Chennai. A CPM-led union had been awaiting a dispute negotiation with the management for about ten months when the DMK leader along with the labour welfare officer got a new union registered which promptly reached a settlement.

'Out of 400 workers, 274 signed individual declarations that the settlement was illegal but this was of no avail. A high proportion of the labour in the factory were unconfirmed and their reluctance to displease the ruling party was effectively exploited,' she writes.

The DMK's heavy-handedness and use of police force was also evident in the case of the strike by workers at the Kauveri Spinning Mills, whose management wanted to add extra workload on the workers in violation of the earlier agreement. The mill owners locked the striking workers out and laid them off. For one year, nothing happened. Sivaraman records what happened during that time: 'It turned out that during the negotiations to get the mill re-started the management wanted the workers to accept a reduction of Rs 50 in Dearness Allowance (DA) as a condition for reopening. When the workers rejected this blackmail, the Labour Commissioner put forward a compromise proposal – a reduction of Rs 40 in DA.' The DMK and Congress unions accepted the settlement while the communists rejected it vehemently.[18]

In 1968, police resorted to firing at striking workers at the Manali Oil Refinery and at the Wimco factory. The strike at the Madras Rubber Factory (MRF) in April 1971 proved to be a litmus test for the Karunanidhi government, whose focus it was to woo investments and foreign trade to the young state. Strong communist unions at the MRF factory struck work for ninety-seven days. The workers, along with their comrades from other industries, painted the city of Madras with red flags as over 10,000 of them marched towards the seat of power at Fort St George. Fighting for better wages, the MRF union, under the leadership of the militant communist trade union leader R. Kuchelar, negotiated hard with the MRF management in an effort to bring down the productivity-linked incentives of workers and increase their fixed wages instead.

As talks continued between the MRF management and the union, with the state government as mediator, a ban order on the strike was issued in July 1971. Sivaraman recounts how 'the next day, the workers of MRF and the other industries in the Thiruvottiyur area, numbering about 10,000, struck work and took out a procession to the Fort St George to protest the ban'.[19]

A curfew order was passed a little after midnight and assembled workers at the factory were picked up in police vans and transported to the distant villages of 'Ponneri, Konderpalayam and Aruppampatti', according to Sivaraman.

She writes of the devious move by the DMK government to ensure that there was no loss of face to the state, which was peddling itself as an investment destination for industries with a cheap and trouble-free labour force. 'All that the government wanted was one single night – a couple of hours – to transport the Seerani Padai and some thugs to the factory so that the morning press reported that "large numbers of workers reported to work" ... In police vans came the strike-breakers, less than 100 of them who became the management's house guests for the next 15 days. Each one was given Rs 100 and entertained to sumptuous feasts, free flow of liquor and movie shows. In return they cleared up the 3 months old cobwebs and helped keep up the myth of the "reopened" factory.'[20]

A massive protest shook Madras city as 50,000 workers descended in support of their MRF brethren. Top union leaders were arrested and branded as 'Naxalites'. The DMK incited the 'Tamil worker' against the 'Malayalee worker'. All of it was in vain. The struggle continued until the MRF management buckled under unrelenting pressure and an agreement was signed in

November 1971, fulfilling the demands of the workers of the factory.

A prominent trade union leader, V.P. Chintan, was attacked murderously by DMK's goons in July 1973. An office-bearer of the Simpson union, Chintan was travelling in a government bus when twenty thugs – DMK workers – stopped it in the middle of a busy road, drove out other passengers and the driver and proceeded to attack Chintan with 'knife, sticks, iron pipes and cycle chains. One of the stab injuries pierced through Chintan's lung, but fortunately Chintan survived the attack after an emergency operation lasting three and a half hours'.[21]

All of this was for two reasons: economic and political. The DMK's biggest political threat at the time was from the communists, who had gained in strength since the 1940s in various parts of Tamil Nadu. They had to be stopped and, for that, their grassroots unions had to be broken up. As for the economy, Karunanidhi had to show numbers – industry had to set up shop in Tamil Nadu for the state to prosper. He managed to achieve both of his goals – with a lot of heartache, bloodshed and atrocity left behind in the wake.

THE EMERGENCY

And then came the Emergency. In 1975, Prime Minister Indira Gandhi took the nation by storm by declaring a national Emergency as the Allahabad High Court delivered a verdict cancelling her re-election. Police repression began in earnest across the country and voices of opposition to Gandhi were muted. Karunanidhi, as chief minister, took an ideological and strident stand against the Emergency despite being an ally.

As Karunanidhi's criticism continued tirelessly, an enraged Gandhi imposed the draconian Maintenance of Internal Securities

Act (MISA) through the governor and dissolved the DMK government in February 1976. Many senior leaders of the party were forced underground. Many others were arrested and tortured in jail.

On the fortieth anniversary of the imposition of the Emergency in June 2015, Stalin gave me an interview, published in the *Hindustan Times*, on his experience during those days. 'The MISA was brought into force in 1975 as soon as Emergency was declared,' he said. 'Leaders like [L.K.] Advani and George Fernandes were arrested and Jayaprakash Narayan started a large movement opposing the Emergency. At that time, Prime Minister Indira Gandhi sent two messengers to Madras to meet our leader Kalaignar.'

Stalin, who was twenty-three at the time of the Emergency, recollected that Gandhi's messengers informed Karunanidhi he did not need to support the Emergency but that he must not oppose it openly.

'If you do not oppose it, your regime shall continue in Tamil Nadu, but if you do oppose it, we will have to dismiss your government – this was the message from Mrs Gandhi,' said Stalin. 'Our leader told them categorically that he was a student of Periyar and Annadurai and that under no circumstances would he ever support dictatorship. He told them that the DMK would always stand for democracy and sent them away.'

Following this, Karunanidhi met Congress leader Kamaraj, a strong opponent of Indira Gandhi, to discuss the political scenario at the Centre and whether his government should resign in protest.

'Kamaraj told Kalaignar that the country is finished,' said Stalin. 'In the whole of India it is only in Tamil Nadu that one can still breathe the air of democracy. Kamaraj told our leader not to resign under any pretext.'

The DMK went on to hold a massive rally at the Marina Beach in Madras, protesting against the imposition of Emergency and demanding that political prisoners be released immediately.

'The very next day, on 31 January 1976, the DMK government was dismissed by the Centre,' said Stalin. 'The police came the same day to Kalaignar's house and asked for Murasoli Maran and for myself. Kalaignar told the police that Maran was in Delhi and that I was campaigning in Madurantakam and that he would hand us both over to police when we returned. The next day both Maran and I went to the police in Madras and were arrested.'

Brutality followed, with violence being unleashed on 500-odd DMK leaders who were arrested with Maran and Stalin.

'Under MISA, we could not approach the courts for relief. It was a draconian act,' said Stalin. 'Maran, former state Electricity Minister Arcot Veerasamy and I were all lodged in jail. Many were forced to sign letters stating that they were not DMK members any more. When we resisted, we were attacked brutally. The life convicts were made to beat all of us badly – this went on for three months,' said Stalin.

DMK MP Chitti Babu died in that attack within the walls of a Madras prison. Arcot Veerasamy lost his hearing in one ear and Maran sustained a back injury that would never heal completely.

Stalin pointed to a scar on his right arm. 'This is one injury that I got when in jail,' he smiled. 'Whenever anyone asks me how I got that, I tell them it is a MISA scar.'

'Kalaignar has been criticized several times by his political rivals for bringing me, his son, into politics,' added Stalin. 'But Kalaignar always replied – I may have brought Stalin into politics but the person who made him a real politician was Indira Gandhi,' he laughed.[22]

But Tamil Nadu did not think much of the DMK's and Karunanidhi's ideological stand with respect to the Emergency. In the election that followed, in 1977, the state chose to place its faith in the matinee idol who had captivated them for years on the large screen – M.G. Ramachandran. MGR swept to power with 144 out of 234 seats. He would remain chief minister for as long as he was alive – until 24 December 1987.

4

CHIEF MINISTER KARUNANIDHI

MGR had successfully discredited the DMK and Karunanidhi in the run-up to the elections in 1977. His campaign revolved around the Sarkaria Commission report and its interim findings which stated that Karunanidhi and his ministers had indeed indulged in corrupt practices and favoured those close to them in various schemes initiated during their tenure.

Women swooned over MGR. Men too were no exception. The Dalit community, having watched their matinee idol on screen, was convinced that MGR alone was their messiah who could deliver them from grinding poverty. A state, collectively in love, voted for one man, no matter who his local representatives were.

MGR remained in power for as long as he was alive, winning three consecutive polls – one election was precipitated due to his government being dismissed by Prime Minister Indira Gandhi.

As Tamil Nadu remained mesmerized by MGR, he too played his part well – his image of a rich man who was the saviour of the poor, hungry, illiterate masses was reiterated by his schemes. MGR picked up former Chief Minister K. Kamaraj's idea of the Mid-Day Nutritious Noon Meal Scheme for children studying in government schools. As per this scheme, children would get hot, cooked lunch at school every day. The idea was to improve the enrolment of children in schools by poor parents who would otherwise send their wards to work. MGR's government expanded the scheme and ensured its effective implementation – from the original 56.9 lakh rural schoolchildren, MGR's government in 1982 extended the scheme to cover 65.7 lakh children, including in the urban areas.

'Attendance at primary schools would go up to 96.2 per cent among the six to eleven age group and to 66.03 per cent in the eleven to fourteen age group.'[1]

So popular was the scheme that successive governments added on to it. Today, few remember that the original scheme was conceived by Kamaraj – 'noon meal scheme', in public memory, belongs to MGR.

R. Kannan writes of MGR's first tenure as chief minister in his biography of the film star:

> A personalized style of politics and administration marked MGR's regime. He was clearly his own man and, until his party's defeat in the January 1980 parliamentary polls, behaved like a pharaoh ... MGR's 'native wisdom and ability to quickly grasp the essentials' impressed bureaucrats. He also quickly got over the shortcoming of his unfamiliarity with English. However, reflecting MGR's inexperience, the performance of his government in its first years was somewhat amateurish ... His accent was on the rural poor.[2]

MGR appeared to be more concerned about his image as a clean and pro-poor chief minister than about actual administration. His welfare schemes were many – apart from the expansion of the noon meal scheme, he provided free toothpowder for children and free footwear. He also promised a job per family.[3] He was also a staunch supporter of the LTTE and was rumoured to have given the militant group Rs 4 crore. Karunanidhi, on the other hand, whose dislike for the LTTE's militancy was evident, would bear the brunt of the group's violent acts on Tamil Nadu soil.

MGR's biggest contribution to Tamil Nadu was in the education sector. It was during his tenure that the Pre-University Course or PUC was replaced with eleventh and twelfth standard classes. Entry of the private sector into the field of education was encouraged, providing rural students with greater access to quality education. Tamil Nadu thus became a hub for educational excellence as large state-of-the-art private colleges and schools were set up.

But ill health and long hospital stays kept MGR away from the seat of power. In 1987, he succumbed to poor health.

With the death of MGR came a window of opportunity for the DMK and Karunanidhi, who had worked tirelessly while in the Opposition to discredit the ruling party, which by then was renamed as the All India Anna Dravida Munnetra Kazhagam (AIADMK). The AIADMK itself was split into two, with one faction led by MGR's wife Janaki Ramachandran and the other led by the charismatic Jayalalithaa Jayaram, a young cine star who had proven her mettle in electoral politics. A battle for the two-leaves election symbol of the AIADMK raged between the two factions, and Janaki won a confidence vote in the assembly as Jayalalithaa's faction boycotted the vote.

Janaki, though, would be chief minister for less than a month, from 7 to 30 January 1988. The Rajiv Gandhi-led Congress government at the Centre dismissed her government citing violence and disruption in the assembly during the trust vote proceedings. President's Rule was imposed on the state and fresh polls were called for in 1989.

The DMK came to power once again, winning 169 out of 234 seats. But this victory was short-lived. The Chandra Shekhar government at the Centre, in 1990, dismissed the DMK government over alleged links with the extremist LTTE, and President's Rule was once again imposed on the state until elections in 1991.

The 1989 elections had witnessed Janaki Ramachandran's faction, contesting under the two-doves symbol, winning a single seat, while Jayalalithaa's faction, contesting under the cock symbol, had won twenty-seven seats. The Election Commission had frozen the two-leaves symbol of the party due to the acrimonious contest between both factions. Janaki Ramachandran conceded defeat and both factions of the party merged in February 1989, restoring the two-leaves symbol to the AIADMK under Jayalalithaa.

A united AIADMK under Jayalalithaa managed to come to power and she became chief minister for the very first time.

From then up until 2011 was a period of alternating rule – Tamil Nadu's voters would swing from the AIADMK to the DMK and back every five years, with a handful of parties added to the mix. The Congress continued to lose ground in the elections, forced to ally with either Dravidian giant.

In 1996, Karunanidhi swept back to power as chief minister, largely thanks to the voters' revulsion at Jayalalithaa's foster son's ostentatious wedding in 1995. The wedding of V.N. Sudhakaran, a nephew of Jayalalithaa's close friend and aide Sasikala Natarajan (who now prefers to be known as V.K. Sasikala), to the granddaughter of cine star Sivaji Ganesan was written about even by the *New York Times* for its grandeur bordering on vulgarity:

> One of India's leading film-set designers was summoned to make whole avenues in central Madras into a tableau of Tamil mythology. For miles between Jayalalithaa's official residence and the wedding site, streets were decorated with pillared castles decorated with Grecian statues and gilded lions. Shrines were erected, with icon-like images of Jayalalithaa in place of Hindu Gods. Fountains played, and the turmoil of daily street life was hidden from view by walls of banana leaves.[4]

Corruption allegations and a perception of high-handedness abounded, and the electorate went back to their old faithful, Kalaignar. Jayalalithaa herself suffered a humiliating defeat in Bargur in Krishnagiri district, from where she contested. The DMK, in alliance with G.K. Moopanar's Tamil Maanila Congress, the Communist Party of India and the All India Forward Bloc, mopped up 221 out of 234 seats in the assembly.

Politics of vengeance soon began, with the Directorate of Vigilance and Anti Corruption (DVAC) under the Karunanidhi government filing a slew of corruption cases against Jayalalithaa and Sasikala. Jayalalithaa in her subsequent term as chief minister would order that Karunanidhi be picked up from his bed after midnight and taken to jail over an alleged flyover scam.

It was in 1996 that Karunanidhi, like his mentor Annadurai who had renamed Madras State as Tamil Nadu in 1969, changed the city of Madras to Chennai, a revised version of Chennapattinam, the original name of the habitation that had sprung up along Marina Beach.

It was also during the 1996–2001 term, though, that Karunanidhi did his best work as chief minister, wooing industry, putting in place welfare policies that benefited the state enormously and brought Tamil Nadu to the top of the list of states in the country in terms of all socio-economic indicators. Of the key welfare schemes, the universal Public Distribution System (PDS) has been an unequivocal success.

Although the state had a history of welfare schemes put in place by the Congress government since before Independence, it was in 1996 that the DMK implemented a key poll promise of rice at Rs 2 per kg through the PDS. Kerosene (for cooking) and sugar too began to be made available at heavily subsidized rates through ration shops under the PDS. From May 2007, in Karunanidhi's next term, wheat, pulses and palmolein too came under the PDS.

The difference between Tamil Nadu's PDS system and those of other states is that subsidized products are available to all and not just the poor. Different sets of ration cards are distributed to the populace – rice card, sugar card and white card. The rice card holder has access to all commodities available in ration shops at subsidized rates. The sugar card holder has access to all commodities, except for rice; instead, she gets three extra kilos of sugar. The white card holder gets no commodities but can use the ration card as proof of address and identity. As of 2011, 94 per cent of the ration cards were rice cards, 5.4 per cent were sugar cards, and white and khaki cards were 0.4 per cent each. Khaki cards are for police personnel only.[5]

A number of experts have analysed the reasons as to why Tamil Nadu's universal PDS has worked so well. A 2010 article in the *Hindu* throws light on the enormous bureaucratic effort that has gone into making the universal PDS work:

> The success of the scheme in Tamil Nadu relies heavily on groundwork. The mammoth task of minimising diversion and reaching 317,000 tonnes of rice to more than 1.97 crore cardholders who draw rations from about 31,439 outlets in 32 districts (including the newly formed Ariyalur and Tiruppur) involves technological interventions, drawing up innovative

fool-proof delivery mechanisms, old-fashioned policing, surprise checks and constant reviews, and fixing responsibility at each level.

The movement of stock from the 310 warehouses across the State to the PDS outlets begins from the 20th of the preceding month (August 20 for September, for instance). By the end of the month, 60 per cent of stocks for the next month reach the PDS outlets. By the 5th of the month of issue, the whole quota reaches the shops. At any given point in time, Tamil Nadu maintains six months' supply of rice, wheat, and other commodities in its warehouses. The movement from the warehouses to the PDS outlets is through trucks – which are tightly controlled by route charts. The charts display the route the truck has to adhere to, details of commodities it carries, and the shop to which the goods are to be delivered. Any elected representative or government official who notices any deviation from the route is authorised to check the vehicle and report to the nearest police station.

Control rooms have been opened in all districts, including in Chennai, to receive information on diversion of PDS commodities. As a trial measure, a GPS-based vehicle movement monitoring system has been implemented in Thiruvallur and Krishnagiri districts to track the movement of vehicles carrying PDS goods. Similarly the State Government has introduced an online godown monitoring system for enabling online capture of all transactions in warehouses in a phased manner. To prevent mass diversion of goods by lorry drivers, every vehicle is accompanied by a department assistant who is provided with a special SIM card attached to a BSNL tower and through this the movement of the vehicle can be tracked from the control room in the Civil Supplies Corporation.

Further, SMS-based fair price shop stock monitoring has been set up by the Cooperative Department to track the stock of every commodity at each fair price shop on a daily basis. This enables officials to identify stock levels at each shop every day and move stocks swiftly as needed. Under the present network, it is possible to identify a shop that may be involved in diversion of stocks by keeping tabs on sudden increases in rice offtake in a month. When there is an abnormal increase in the offtake, vigilance teams swing into action to find out whether the increased offtake is genuine or bogus.

Handheld billing machines with a GPRS connection have been installed in all fair price shops in Chennai to enable real-time monitoring of sales and stocks. A usual complaint of cardholders is short measurement and to avoid this fair price shops are being supplied electronic weighing machines. In the present setup, cardholders can register their complaints against the shopkeeper through an online service.

A majority of fair price shops in the State are run by the Cooperative Department. In fact, Tamil Nadu is the only State where fair price outlets are run either by the Government or by its agencies. This system has proved to be advantageous since the wholesaler is a government corporation and all the retail shops are either Government-run cooperatives or under the control of the Civil Supplies Department. Most shops run on a loss. The Government routinely provides about Rs 300 crore as subsidy to run the Cooperative shops (to cover establishment costs, wages, etc).[6]

But leakage and corruption do take place, as in any other state. The disadvantages of universal PDS as against targeted PDS too stack up against the scheme.

Tamil Nadu has a recurring subsidy burden of Rs 4,500 crore, which is almost 5 per cent of its annual expenditure. Justice

> Wadhwa Committee had even questioned its financial viability in the long run. In a system of universal coverage of PDS, if better-off sections of the population utilize the PDS and do not exclude themselves voluntarily, then these sections experience an income transfer at the cost of large subsidies for the government.
>
> Universal coverage of the PDS in Tamil Nadu also reduces the entitlements of the poor. All households in Tamil Nadu (except those with AAY cards) can receive a maximum of 25 kg of food grains (20 kg of rice and 5 kg of wheat). But BPL households are entitled to 35 kg of food grains in other states. Thus, Tamil Nadu has been able to adopt the universal system by spreading thinner the central allocations to the state under the BPL category.
>
> Also, the per capita entitlement of the poor is lower than the rich since there is an upper limit to the entitlements per household and average size of poor households is higher than that of non-poor. The poor then resort to buying grains from better-off sections who sell their entitlements at a price higher than PDS price but lower than the market price, thus making a profit out of the subsidized grains allotted to them.[7]

With the implementation of the Food Security Act from 2017 onwards, Tamil Nadu stands to take on an additional burden of Rs 1,730 crore, as the AIADMK government has promised to continue universal PDS despite the Centre's quota of contribution reducing drastically.

THE 2000s

The period from 2001 to 2006 was Jayalalithaa's turn in the sun, and this tenure saw a more nuanced and mature chief minister. She had learnt her lessons from the wedding debacle and embraced austerity in dress and appearance.

This tenure saw the AIADMK government focus on the development of the state and its industrial economy. Tamil Nadu was at the forefront on all indicators – the state was power surplus, the treasury was brimming and health indicators were soaring. The flagship Muthulakshmi Reddy maternal benefit scheme, which was initially introduced by the AIADMK government in 1987, was taken forward by the DMK government between 1996 and 2001. In 2001, Jayalalithaa doubled the assistance given to pregnant and lactating mothers to Rs 12,000 and helped increase institutional deliveries in the state. This benefits, on average, 6.5 lakh mothers in Tamil Nadu.

It was between 1996 and 2001, experts claim, that both the DMK and the AIADMK governments did their best work in terms of governance and important welfare schemes, which benefited the cause of social justice.

But Jayalalithaa also erred. Her autocratic move to slap the draconian ESMA (Essential Services Maintenance Act) on 1.7 lakh striking government employees in 2003 cost her electorally in 2006. Although she reinstated the staff, they would not forget, nor forgive, come poll time. Jayalalithaa also ordered a ban on animal sacrifice in the state in 2003. Widespread outrage forced her to go back on her move and repeal the ban the next year. It was too late, though.

Jayalalithaa was defeated by a clever political manouevre by bête noire Karunanidhi in 2006. In what seemed an otherwise 'issue-less' election, Karunanidhi was at his tactical best – stitching together a rainbow coalition of caste-based parties such as the Pattali Makkal Katchi (PMK) as well as the Left parties and the Congress.

On the eve of the poll, the DMK released its astounding manifesto – free colour televisions would be given to the BPL population if they voted the alliance into power. A state fed and bred on cinema and television was enamoured. Karunanidhi was back in the chief minister's seat.

This time, he was a man in a hurry. Perhaps he knew in his gut that this would be his last term as chief minister of his beloved state. Or maybe he realized that the win over the AIADMK was a slim one – the DMK had just about managed to scrape through. Perhaps he could foretell the future – his own health would deteriorate suddenly and drastically by 2016, rendering him speechless and reliant on machines and tubes for life.

Between 2006 and 2011, a large number of schemes were announced. The state spent heavily on building a grand new Secretariat building and Asia's largest library, the Anna Centenary Library, in Kotturpuram, Chennai. He also introduced Samacheer Kalvi – Tamil Nadu's unique syllabus that promised uniform and equitable education to all – the Kalaignar Health Insurance Scheme for the poor, and exclusive reservation within the backward caste quota for Muslims as well as reservation for Arundhathiyars within the scheduled caste quota.

This was also the tenure when the term 'welfare state' was taken to new levels. A sum of Rs 4,000 crore was spent on giving away free colour television sets. Along with this began a new phase of media manipulation in Tamil Nadu. Karunanidhi attempted to revive Arasu Cable, a state-owned cable television distribution network that offered at low cost a bouquet of television channels that could be watched on Kalaignar's colour television sets. Launched in July 2008, Arasu Cable (meaning Government Cable) was intended to be a direct hit at the Maran brothers – Kalanidhi and Dayanidhi, media baron and MP respectively – who had offended the Karunanidhi family by publishing a controversial opinion poll about who would succeed Karunanidhi. Arasu Cable was Karunanidhi's way of putting the powerful brothers in their place by undercutting the monopoly of the Kalanidhi Maran-owned SCV or Sumangali Cable Vision, the largest cable distributor in the state with the widest network. But more on the family feuds later.

SAMACHEER KALVI

A poll promise by the DMK about improving the quality of education in Tamil Nadu resulted in a carefully crafted and forward-looking scheme that came to be called Samacheer Kalvi, or State Platform for Common School System.

Work began on this project almost immediately after Karunanidhi was sworn in as chief minister in 2006. A junior first-time minister, Thangam Thennarasu, was put in charge of formulating the scheme that would affect lakhs of school students across the state.

'Tamil Nadu, until then, had different systems of education, each with a different syllabus, different patterns of examination and different marks,' explains Thangam Thennarasu. 'There was a big disparity in existence. Thalaivar [our leader] told me that we need to bring in parity in education as there was a clear divide between the students studying in remote rural areas and those in urban areas. Education must be uniform for everyone and quality education must be made available to everyone, irrespective of whether they study in government schools or private schools. That was the concept of Samacheer Kalvi.'

In Tamil Nadu, before Samacheer Kalvi, various streams of education existed – state board, matriculation, Anglo Indian, Oriental as well as the Centre's CBSE (Central Board of Secondary Education) and ICSE (Indian Certificate of Secondary Education) streams.

While CBSE and ICSE were largely preferred by urban upper-middle-class families, the two most popular syllabi were state board – that covered the rural poor in government schools – and matriculation – which was seen as a step up from state board but not as good as CBSE or ICSE. The matriculation syllabus was taught by private schools which were popular across the state.

'There was a popular perception, which was also true to an extent, that the private matriculation schools were better than the government schools,' says Thennarasu. 'But it was also leading to commercial exploitation as a result by these schools. That was the reason this whole process of Samacheer Kalvi started. The idea was that even the union school in a small village should offer the same quality of education as the top notch schools in Chennai.'

A team of experts was formed and a detailed survey and analysis of content of the varied syllabi conducted. What the expert team found was that there was a gap of one year between the state board and the matriculation syllabi. For instance, a student studying in the sixth standard in a matriculation school would study the same only in the seventh standard in a state board school.

The idea was to bring the syllabi on a par with the CBSE syllabus. 'But if we introduced a CBSE-like syllabus suddenly, the students in the rural areas would not be able to cope. So we decided to upgrade the syllabus phase by phase and ease students into the change. Samacheer is a process and we had to start at some point,' says Thennarasu.

The opposition was vehement. The new syllabus was challenged on the grounds that it was substandard and politically loaded. For instance, images of a rising sun, the DMK's electoral symbol, were cannily inserted into the new textbooks. There were chapters singing Karunanidhi's praises and crowing the DMK's achievements.

When the government changed in 2011, Jayalalithaa scrapped Samacheer Kalvi, stating that the quality of the curriculum was poor. Samacheer subsequently turned into a court battle, with the Supreme Court in 2011 finally allowing the curriculum to be implemented in the state but also giving the government leeway to delete the objectionable political content in the textbooks. Teachers and parents slogged away, sticking paper on to DMK symbols, Karunanidhi's achievements, and pictures of the statue of Tiruvalluvar, which was used as the logo for a World Tamil Conference.[8]

NEW SECRETARIAT AND ANNA CENTENARY LIBRARY

Thennarasu was also handed two key projects by the DMK chief – one was to oversee the construction of the ambitious new Secretariat at a cost of Rs 1,200 crore. Karunanidhi laid the foundation stone for the new building at Omandurar Estate near Marina Beach in 2008 and Prime Minister Manmohan Singh inaugurated the premises in March 2010.

On the day of the inauguration, though, the dome of the assembly building was not yet ready. Thennarasu came up with an ingenious plan – to create a temporary dome for the inauguration of Karuna's pet project and complete the final construction subsequently.

Art director Thotta Tharani was called in and an artificial dome was created at a cost of Rs 3 crore out of the public exchequer, drawing much flak from the media and public for wasteful expenditure. Within a year of the inauguration, elections arrived and the AIADMK swept to power with a vast majority. The grand new Secretariat became a multi-speciality hospital and the permanent dome cost the new government Rs 6.86 crore to build.[9]

KALAIGNAR HEALTH INSURANCE SCHEME

In 2009, Karunanidhi came out with a much lauded scheme that aimed at making healthcare more affordable to the poor. Falling short of being a universal free healthcare scheme, the Kalaignar Kappeettu Thittam was targeted at 1 crore families, providing medical insurance cover to the tune of Rs 1 lakh to each. Called the 'Kalaignar Insurance Scheme for Life Saving Treatments', this scheme assured the card holder complete cashless treatment for the amount insured. The government would pay the insurance premium of Rs 500 per annum, and close to Rs 1,500 crore was spent on the scheme.

While all medical procedures were not covered under the insurance scheme, important surgeries such as the heart bypass surgery were.

So successful was this scheme that Jayalalithaa, who came to power next in 2011, contrary to her usual strategy of disbanding all of Karunanidhi's schemes, kept it going, although with its name changed to 'Chief Minister's Comprehensive Insurance Scheme' and expanded the list of medical procedures from fifty-one to eighty-nine.

Karunanidhi's 2006–11 tenure was also notorious for large-scale land grabbing and loot of public money that the DMK's regional strongmen allegedly indulged in. Karunanidhi, it seems, had lost control of the party as regional leaders like E.V. Velu of Tiruvannamalai, K.N. Nehru of Trichy, the late Veerapandi Arumugam of Salem and I. Periasamy of Dindigul grew far too powerful within the party, and Karunanidhi, perhaps, far too dependent on them for electoral victories.

'If Thalaivar came to know of any issue, he would never tolerate it,' says Thennarasu. 'He could not monitor every functionary. But as far as the government was concerned, he would brook no fault or wrongdoing. If he felt any space would be misused, he would stop it.'

The *Hindu*'s N. Ram too feels that Karunanidhi and the DMK's undoing in this tenure was the leader's poor judgement. 'I think his biggest flaw was to allow some undesirable elements to be there and to stand by them,' he says, while clarifying that he does not include former Union Telecom Minister A. Raja and key accused in the 2G case in that list.

The final tenure of Muthuvel Karunanidhi as Chief Minister of Tamil Nadu would see him enmeshed in controversies like the 2G scandal, fending off internecine rivalry and reining in his furious elder son M.K. Alagiri.

OVERVIEW

In the final analysis, Tamil Nadu has fared better under the two mighty Dravidian parties than most other states in India, save Maharashtra and Gujarat. The large state's economy continues to chug faster than the country's on average, every year. Growth and governance are largely stable. And Tamil Nadu's administration and policies are pioneering, followed by the rest of the states in India as well as by the Central government.

In a keen comparison of Uttar Pradesh and Tamil Nadu, a 2013 research paper by Samuel Paul and Kala Seetharam Sridhar throws light on why Tamil Nadu has been able to move ahead at a furious pace compared to the northern state:

> TN led the country in the reservation policy in education that others emulated in later periods. More importantly, the social movements that dominated TN politics and public discourse in the early part of the 20th century created a much greater awareness among the lower castes that constituted the majority

of the population about their rights and the need for collective action to claim their entitlements.

Scholars who have documented social movements across India have pointed out that similar movements did not occur in UP or other northern states. In both regions, there were movements that protested caste abuses and brahminical dominance. But the distinguishing feature of the TN social movements was their focus on gaining access to education and economic opportunities such as jobs in government. These movements not only created greater awareness among the backward classes about the need for collective struggles to achieve their ends, but also increased their sense of solidarity and mutual trust among the members, and helped them create vast new networks to mobilize resources and launch collective political and social action to achieve common ends. It was thus that large numbers of schools, colleges, and in recent years engineering colleges were set up by caste and community supported leaders and groups.

A similar trend has been noted in the industry sector of TN where, again, impressive numbers of small and medium enterprises have been set up by entrepreneurs, who took advantage of their caste and community networks. The governments in power facilitated this process, resulting in a groundswell of private sector development. Among the political leaders who promoted this process in TN were K. Kamaraj, R. Venkataraman, Annadorai and C. Subramaniam. Developments of this kind do not seem to have occurred in UP. The importance of these historical factors, especially social movements, in laying the foundation for strengthening both the demand and supply sides of development in TN cannot be overemphasized.[10]

In the ruins of the day, Karunanidhi, perhaps, could be satisfied that despite all of the politicking, the deterioration of electoral politics and the cut-throat nature of the game, he contributed in large part to Tamil Nadu being a successful and pro-poor state whose policies have been emulated by its neighbours and by states in northern India.

5

FRIEND-TURNED-FOE AND SWORN ENEMY: MGR AND JAYALALITHAA

Anandan, dressed in white pants, a red shirt and a polka-dotted navy-blue scarf flung rakishly around his neck, walks on a vast red oxide floor. The camera moves upwards, revealing a crowd of people rushing to catch a glimpse of him as he peeps over the parapet wall. He stares, perplexed at the crowd.

A hand grabs Anandan's and lifts it up in a wave as the crowd surges forward and roars in adulation. Tamilselvan is next to an uncomprehending Anandan.

'This is the power of the people. Lenin, Stalin, Hitler, everyone worked hard to cultivate and get this power. A power that enables one to get close to the people's heart.'

'But,' says Anandan, 'I am just an actor!'

'They don't think so. Look there. They have buried your image deep inside their hearts. They will give their lives for you. What are you going to do with this?' asks Tamilselvan with urgency.

'What should I do?'

Tamilselvan answers him. 'You should not leave it like this. You have to make this 1,000 times bigger. It has to be of benefit to the party's ideology. Everything is in your face and in that [cinema] screen.'

Realization dawns on Anandan. He then waves with both hands, putting one foot on the parapet wall, in his trademark style, as the roar from the crowd below gets louder.

This is one of the most powerful scenes in director Mani Ratnam's much acclaimed *Iruvar*, released in 1997, a film based on the complex friend–foe relationship between Tamil cinema's superstar, M.G. Ramachandran, and Karunanidhi. Anandan is based on MGR and played by Malayalam actor Mohanlal. The character based on Karunanidhi, called Tamilselvan, is played by Prakash Raj, a role that won him the National Award for the Best Supporting Actor in 1998. The film flopped at the box office but the real-life plot on which it was based is riveting.

From camaraderie to opportunism to jealousy to vengeance, along with a deep-rooted affection for each other, the relationship between MGR and Karunanidhi was complicated at best and one of conflict at worst.

THE BEGINNING

In 1944, once Karunanidhi got the go-ahead from Periyar to leave behind his writing and editing duties in *Kudiyarasu* magazine, he agreed to producer A.S.A. Samy's offer to write the screenplay for the film *Rajakumari*. The movie house Jupiter Films had decided to cast a fair, young Malayalee as the lead actor in the film.

Marudur Gopalan Ramachandran, or MGR as he eventually came to be known, was dressed in a khadi shirt with a rudraksha maalai around his neck. An ardent follower of Gandhi and a member of the Congress party, MGR met the young Karunanidhi and they quickly struck up a friendship.

'I would give him books written by Anna. He would give me books by Gandhi. We would debate over these often,' recalls Karunanidhi in *Nenjukku Needhi*.[1]

It is not clear exactly when, but the two, in equal penury, shared a room together in Coimbatore for about four months, and a strong bond developed.

'It was initially a great friendship,' says Duraimurugan, a confidant of Karunanidhi's, although a much younger man. 'In fact, it was MGR who introduced me to Kalaignar when they had come together for a function near my village.'

Duraimurugan recounts that it was in the run-up to the historic by-poll of Tiruvannamalai in 1963 that he first met the man he would come to call his leader. A student at Madras's Pachaiyappa's College and active in the DMK's student wing, Duraimurugan was using his annual vacation to help the party organize election funds through what was called 'sirappu koottam' (special gatherings). The DMK in its early days would often organize such gatherings, charging for tickets to attend the meetings in which popular political leaders like Anna, Karunanidhi, Nedunchezhiyan and MGR would speak. These funds were then used by the candidate of that area to tour and campaign for the polls.

The DMK's candidate in that by-poll was P.U. Shanmugam, and he was going up against a mighty Congress party that ruled the state. At a sirappu koottam at K.V. Kuppam village, about three miles from his home, the young Duraimurugan sat on stage as MGR and Karunanidhi arrived together for the gathering.

MGR recognized the fiery Duraimurugan from an event at Pachaiyappa's College a few months earlier, when the young student had impressed the cine star with a fine welcome address. 'MGR liked my speech and appreciated me when he spoke on stage afterward,' recalls Duraimurugan.

'"What are you doing here?" MGR asked me. I told him I was on vacation and had come to organize the koottam. MGR then asked me to contest for the chairman's post of an Inter College Association, a student body comprising twenty to twenty-five colleges. MGR and I were having an animated discussion when Kalaignar noticed us talking. He asked MGR who I was. That was when MGR introduced me to my leader,' says Duraimurugan. He was around twenty-two years old at the time.

The by-poll would prove to be a historic one – Shanmugam won, defeating the ruling party and setting the stage for the DMK to come to power in the state four years later.

'Their [MGR and Karunanidhi's] friendship was evident at that koottam as they travelled together and addressed rallies together,' says Duraimurugan.

Rewind by a decade and their early days paint a picture of a struggle for survival for both Karunanidhi and MGR.

Karunanidhi would go on to pen the screenplay for the film *Manthiri Kumari*, which released in 1950 and was produced by T.R. Sundaram of Modern Theatres. Karuna, by then an acclaimed film scriptwriter, would recommend the young MGR for a key role in the film. It was a box-office blockbuster and MGR was catapulted to stardom almost overnight.

MGR, who had until then been a member of the Congress and an ardent Gandhian, left the party to join the fledgling DMK in 1953. Annadurai and Karunanidhi saw the potential of using MGR to spread the message of the Dravidian ideology far and wide through film. MGR, basking in his newfound adulation, was only too happy to do so. A series of films followed, almost all super hits, with MGR in the lead and Karunanidhi wielding the pen.

The 'plot' worked in real life too, especially in 1967, strangely through an unforeseen tragic circumstance. This tragedy would also contribute in large measure to the DMK coming to power in the state for the very first time.

On 12 January 1967, as the DMK was preparing for elections in full swing, a meeting took place at MGR's residence in Nandambakkam, Chennai. Having a chat about their next film were MGR and film producer K.K. Vasu. Around 5 p.m., fellow actor M.R. Radha entered MGR's house to join the discussion. Shots were subsequently heard and both MGR and M.R. Radha were rushed to hospital with bullets in their bodies. Not much was known beyond this as the case was hushed up.

According to the *Hindu*, 'The bullet that entered near MGR's left ear had "lodged itself behind the first vertebra". In the case of Radha, one bullet fired at the right temple "had caused an injury and fractured the skull. Another fired in the neck got embedded at the rear part of the neck".'[2]

MGR's fans went on a rampage, vandalizing M.R. Radha's house in Chennai. People came out in droves to pray for their favourite cine idol as he underwent treatment at the Government Hospital in Chennai. Photographs were released and circulated widely of the film star with a bandage around his neck. The bullet was removed from MGR's spine a month later, but his voice was affected for life. A sympathy wave for the wounded MGR swept the state – and carried him and the DMK to power. MGR, true to his penchant for theatrics, took oath in his hospital bed as MLA for the St Thomas Mount constituency.

Karunanidhi probably realized subsequently that MGR was a man to watch, as his popularity amongst the masses was far greater than his own. Self-preservation and ambition on the part of both led to a fracture in friendship and political ties between the two giants of Tamil politics.

'In the first week of August 1972, at the Madurai rally, MGR stated that the party was a flawless home and that the party's government was a clean palace. That same MGR, after sixty days, decided that he would break the party and its government,' writes Karuna, accusing MGR of betrayal.[3]

THE BREAK

In the wake of Annadurai's death, a quick and intense succession battle between his second-in-command Nedunchezhiyan and the young Karunanidhi had seen the latter winning and ascending to the chief minister's chair. At that time, one of the most vocal voices of support in Karunanidhi's favour had been that of his friend MGR, a man adored by millions of cinema goers in the state.

In Mani Ratnam's *Iruvar* is depicted what perhaps took place as the two men set out to fulfil individual ambitions. Karuna, played by Prakash Raj, intense, ideological and a fiery writer, poet and orator, would rouse the crowds at public rallies. But when MGR, played by Mohanlal, made an entry, the crowds went berserk, ignoring Dravidian ideology for a film star who enthralled them. Karunanidhi knew that his biggest rival was one that he himself had nurtured.

Senior journalists in Tamil Nadu speak of how, after Karunanidhi took over from Annadurai as the chief minister, MGR met with him to congratulate him. At the same time, he demanded the post of health minister. Karunanidhi is said to have given the cine star an ultimatum – give up acting if you want to become a minister – knowing full well that MGR's strength was his mass adulation, a result of his on-screen image as a saviour of the people.

Karunanidhi's supporters absolve him of having played politics with his friend. 'It is true that MGR asked for the health ministry,' says Duraimurugan. 'Kalaignar would have given it to him too. But a lot of others, like Law Minister Madhavan and P.U. Shanmugam, advised Kalaignar against giving a minister's post to an actor. Madhavan was completely against it and even cited relevant portions of the law to prove his point.'

But MGR's loyalists differ. 'It is a 100 per cent lie,' says C. Ponnaiyan, MGR's junior lawyer and transport, law and education minister under him. He was also finance minister from 2001 to 2006 in the Jayalalithaa cabinet. 'According to the code of conduct of ministerial service, no minister should hold an office of profit. MGR's passion was for serving the people of Tamil Nadu for social upliftment, for which, he felt, cinema was the best field. So he did not prefer to become a minister by coming out of the cine field.'

Ponnaiyan says that when the DMK first came to power in 1967 under Annadurai's leadership, Anna mentioned in front of him (Ponnaiyan) and others present that since MGR did not prefer to become a minister, they should respect his wishes, as MGR was doing the 'most important work'. 'MGR told Anna that he could be the government or any minister he wanted to be in his films, so he did not need a ministry,' Ponnaiyan says.

He gives another explanation as to what happened during the time the DMK broke into two. 'In 1969, when Anna died, Nedunchezhiyan should have become the chief minister. Anna had told many of us on many occasions. But, for over a decade, Karunanidhi had resorted to various means to gain support from the district secretaries of the party and the subordinate level of the party organizers with the help of MGR and his MGR mandrams (fan clubs). In reality, at that time, Karunanidhi was not a senior leader. It was only with the help of MGR mandrams that he started developing his image,' he says.

Ponnaiyan says that the break between Karunanidhi and MGR happened due to a promise broken by the former. 'MGR got a promise from him [Karunanidhi] that he would run a clean, pro-poor and a welfare-oriented government,' he says. 'But because Karunanidhi failed to adhere to administrative purity during his tenure as chief minister, indulging in notorious scams – like the wheat scandal and the aerial spraying scam – MGR, the party and activists began questioning Karunanidhi's corrupt indulgences. That was the root cause behind MGR's expulsion from the DMK and the birth of the ADMK.'

Whichever version is true, the split did happen. An angry MGR bided his time until 1972, when as party treasurer he raised a shrill voice against one-time mentor Karunanidhi, accusing him of corruption involving party funds. Karunanidhi promptly expelled him from the party. A gleeful MGR left, taking with him one half of the DMK cadre, and formed the Anna Dravida Munnetra Kazhagam (ADMK), which would later become the All India Anna Dravida Munnetra Kazhagam (AIADMK).

How did a politically adept Karunanidhi misjudge the situation so badly and create a rival whom he would not be able to beat as long as he was alive? 'Kalaignar hesitated to remove MGR from the party,' explains Duraimurugan. 'He knew how popular MGR was and he did not want to expel him. But Naavalar [Nedunchezhiyan] was insistent that Karuna expel MGR. Naavalar had his own selfish reasons for this. He wanted to take revenge on MGR, who had been one of the most vociferous supporters of Karunanidhi as chief minister following Anna's death.' He adds that MGR too would not have gone against Karunanidhi if not for his acolytes poisoning his ears against Karuna.

In effect, according to Duraimurugan, the parting of ways of Karunanidhi and MGR was 'a series of unfortunate incidents'.

By 1976, Karunanidhi's government was dismissed on charges of corruption. Karunanidhi had been a vocal opponent of Prime Minister Indira Gandhi's Emergency, which was declared in 1975.

A miffed Mrs Gandhi, whose Congress (R) had the support of the DMK, also realized that MGR was the next big thing in Tamil politics. An alliance between Gandhi and MGR eventually came about in 1977. The rug was pulled from under Karunanidhi's feet as he was charged with corruption and a Commission of Inquiry instituted under Justice Ranjit Singh Sarkaria as its chairman.

> On November 4, 1972, Shri M.G. Ramachandran, M.L.A., of Tamil Nadu State Assembly sent a Memorandum to the President of India praying for the appointment of a Commission of Inquiry
>
> a) Against the entire Cabinet of the Tamil Nadu Government.
> b) Against all the District Secretaries of the ruling Karunanidhi D.M.K.
> c) Against the officials against whom specific charges have been made in the accompanying annexure, and
> d) Against such other officials and such other persons who are involved in abetting with corrupt Ministers and officials.[4]

Apart from MGR, five others had made similar representations to V.V. Giri, President of India, on 6 November 1972. These were forwarded to Prime Minister Gandhi, who forwarded the complaints to Karunanidhi and asked him for his comments.

Between 14 December 1972 and 28 May 1973, a series of letters flew between Madras and Delhi as Gandhi, MGR and Karunanidhi engaged in a battle over corruption allegations. Finally, on 3 February 1976, the Sarkaria Commission of Inquiry was set up.[5]

The allegations of corruption were many, twenty-eight in all. These ranged from irregularities in allocating tenders for government projects, non-payment of tax and also 'smothering of a murder case' to protect a minister.

Karunanidhi's second term in power (1971-76) was a disillusioning one for the people of Tamil Nadu. Corruption set in, with a large number of ministers, MLAs, MPs and local power centres of the DMK earning hitherto unimagined sums of money.

Take, for instance, the case of Anbil Dharmalingam, minister for local administration and agriculture in the Karunanidhi cabinet in its second term. Before becoming a minister on 15 March 1971, Dharmalingam was not an income tax assessee as he simply did not own enough property, wealth or income to be assessed.

Prior to 1967, Anbil Dharmalingam, his brother Ponnurama Nattar, and his sister Dhanamanickam, had only the following properties:

1) Two old houses in Jangamarajapuram
2) Fifty-three cents of Nanja land;
3) Eight acres of wet land (leasehold) at village Anbil.

After the DMK came to power for the very first time under C.N. Annadurai in 1967, however, Anbil Dharmalingam began to get more affluent. Below are a list of properties in his name.

1) 2.16 acres of land worth Rs 10,700 in Mangarnmalpuram Village, purchased on 5th January 1970.
2) A house worth Rs 75,000 at Paramasivapuram in Lalgudi, constructed in 1968 over plot No. C-47 measuring 3,600 square feet purchased on 4th May 1968 for Rs 1,479.83.
3) (a) Ambassador Car No. MDY 9595 purchased on 31st August 1968 and sold on 5th August 1971.
   (b) Ambassador Car No. TNY 999 on hire purchase endorsed by the Bank of India, Tiruchirappalli on 30th June 1971, and sold on 12th September 1972.
   (c) Fiat Car No TNY 3334 purchased on 4th January 1973.

4) (a) Fixed Deposit of Rs 1,000 in the Bank of India.
   (b) Fixed Deposit of Rs 2,000 in State Bank of India, Lalgudi.
   (c) Fixed Deposit of Rs 20,000 in District Central Bank, Tiruchirappalli.
   (d) Jewels worth less than Rs 10,000.[6]

This is only the tip of the iceberg, as per the Sarkaria Commission Report. Wealth and a number of properties had been accumulated in the names of Dharmalingam's relatives, sons and other friends in barely a decade since the DMK tasted power. What was worse, Nathan Publications, in which Dhanamanickam was a partner along with one Kasturi Chettiar, a DMK member, received the deal of printing school textbooks for students in certain districts of Tamil Nadu, a clear conflict of interest. It is also noted with documentary evidence in the Sarkaria Commission Report that Dharmalingam would stay at a room in the Nathan Publications building whenever he visited Trichy. From 1970 to 1976, Nathan Publications increasingly did brisk business despite lower bidders in the same districts with more experience and outlets to sell books, states the report.

Karunanidhi himself was found in the crosshairs, having signed off on murky deals, including on the sale of the Samayanallur Thermal Power Plant, the aerial spraying of pesticides for crops and other such schemes that favoured his cronies.

One-time friend MGR had now turned foe. This would be the bitterest of pills for Karunanidhi to swallow.

'They parted ways but the affection for one another remained the same,' recalls Duraimurugan. 'The Sarkaria Commission final report clearly shows that none of the charges were ultimately proven.'

The AIADMK disagrees. 'The mystery in this is the extraordinary money power of Karunanidhi which made clinching witnesses turn hostile,' says Ponnaiyan. 'When Karunanidhi and team requested Morarji Desai to intervene in the case, he refused to interfere in judicial administration. But subsequently Karunanidhi very trickily made use of the political situation in our country at the time. He was able to wriggle out of strong evidence-based cases,' he says, alluding to the general impression at the time that Karunanidhi had surrendered to Indira Gandhi in order to come clean from the Sarkaria Commission cases, while MGR was seen to be leaning towards Morarji Desai.

Come 1977 and elections arrived once again in the state. MGR went alone in the election to complete a clean sweep of the state. After coming to power, he extended a hand of support to the Janata Party government at the Centre. From 1977 to 1987, MGR remained chief minister, setting a record as the only person to have sat in the seat in the state for two terms in succession. This despite the Centre dismissing his government in 1980 as national politics took a turn, with Indira Gandhi coming back to power and siding with the DMK again. But the subsequent assembly elections returned him to power – this time in an alliance with the redoubtable Indira Gandhi. His successor Jayalalithaa would accomplish consecutive wins much later, in 2011 and 2016, but would not live to complete the second term.

KARUNANIDHI FIGHTS BACK

A thumping defeat it may have been but Karunanidhi would not be down for long. As leader of the Opposition in the state assembly, he would fight back – and in style.

Assembly proceedings of 1979 are evidence of the power of oratory as well as the keenness of research that Karunanidhi is well known for. In an eighty-five-minute speech in the state assembly that put his old friend MGR in a sticky spot, Karunanidhi ripped into the ADMK government's claims of a corruption-free administration by pointing to the unorthodox allocation of medical seats, which the Madras High Court had earlier torn down as 'arbitrary'. He also provided documentary proof of a 'shipping scam' in which a whistleblower IAS officer was punished.

India Today, in December 1979, published the details of the 'shipping scam' unearthed by Karunanidhi:

> The Tamil Nadu Government floated Poompuhar Shipping Corporation in 1975 to transport coal to its thermal power plants. It acquired two ships, Tamil Anna from a Japanese firm and Tamil Periyar from a Birla company. After incurring heavy losses, both the ships were scrapped. In 1976, when the state was under President's rule, it was decided to wind up the corporation.
>
> Came the MGR Ministry the year after and it was determined to keep the corporation afloat, recurring losses notwithstanding. Poompuhar negotiated with Bulgaria for the purchase of three ships of 38,000 DWT each, to be financed by the Government of India's shipping development fund. The Bulgarian firm offered the ships at Rs 8.4 crore each.
>
> Underhand Dealings: The Tamil Nadu Government, instead, negotiated the deal through a broker who belonged to the charmed circle of MGR cronies to buy them at Rs 10.4 crore each, with a view to cornering the difference as commission, the lion's share going to MGR, said Karunanidhi. Producing 16 papers, including copies of telex messages and letters as documentary evidence, Karunanidhi said the team of officials who went to Bulgaria to finalise the deal and sign the contract, settled for a lower price, unaware of the underhand dealings entered into through the broker.
>
> Irked by this unexpected turn of events, the Government decided to defer the deal, and advised the Shipping Development

> Fund Committee in Delhi accordingly. Tocho Tochev, the Bulgarian Ambassador in Delhi, who was to inaugurate a Bulgarian-Tamil Nadu friendship association in Madras to coincide with the delivery of the first ship, called off his visit to the city.
>
> K.S. Ramakrishnan, the IAS officer, who was managing director of Poompuhar Shipping Corporation, a member of the official team to Bulgaria, and responsible for detecting the conspiracy, found to his dismay that instead of being patted on the back for a job well done, he was being relieved of his post. Jid Singh Bhango, another IAS official included in the team to Bulgaria, died suddenly in Madras under suspicious circumstances. H. N. Singh, the third member, also belonging to the IAS, and presently Home Secretary to the State Government, is about to be shunted to an innocuous assignment.[7]

In the ten years that Karunanidhi led the Opposition, he never let MGR rest. But the affection of many decades stayed.

AIADMK leaders speak of two incidents that showed them clearly how MGR respected his arch rival. Kulandaivelu, an AIADMK leader, was once slapped by MGR when he mentioned the name Karunanidhi. 'Who are you to call him by his name? What status have you got? He is my thalaivar [leader] and I myself call him Kalaignar,' MGR is said to have chastised him.

Another instance was when MGR was travelling in a car on a highway along with some of his trusted acolytes. Jeppiar, who went on to become a liquor and education baron, was amongst the passengers. Jeppiar is said to have used foul words to describe Karunanidhi, following which a furious MGR stopped the car and made Jeppiar get out and walk back to Chennai.

DMK leaders too have tales to tell of the fondness and respect that Karunanidhi had for MGR. Duraimurugan recounts how in

1985-86, when MGR was the chief minister, Madras University decided to honour him with a doctorate. But there was a hitch – Duraimurugan was a member of the syndicate of the Madras University and all honorary doctorates had to be approved by the syndicate. Even one veto would mean the doctorate would not be given.

'Thinking that I will not agree to MGR getting the doctorate, the principal quietly organized everything. His plan was that a few hours before MGR arrived, he would quickly get the syndicate to sign off and approve the doctorate. But I heard about this plan the night before. So around 1 a.m., I went to Kalaignar's house and woke him up to tell him what was afoot,' says Duraimurugan.

'Kalaignar told me, "There is no enmity between me and MGR. Only a difference of opinion. Don't oppose the doctorate which is being given to him for his good deeds."'

On the advice of his leader, early the next morning, to the astonishment of the principal, Duraimurugan himself proposed the honorary doctorate for MGR at the syndicate and approved it unanimously.

By 1984, though, MGR fell seriously ill. On 5 October 1984, the chief minister, gasping for breath, was admitted to Apollo Hospital in Chennai. As his condition worsened, experts were flown in from the US and Japan to treat him. His kidneys had failed him and, in order to get a transplant, he was flown to the Downstate Medical Center in Brooklyn, New York, on 5 November 1984. A little over a month later, on 19 December, he underwent a kidney transplant, thanks to his niece who donated one of hers.

As Tamil Nadu prayed for the recovery of their beloved chief minister, Prime Minister Indira Gandhi was assassinated on 31 October 1984 and her son Rajiv Gandhi took over. A decision was taken jointly with V.R. Nedunchezhiyan, MGR's finance minister, who was handling the chief minister's portfolios, to hold elections early – by December 1984. MGR lay in a hospital bed in New York but won the election from Andipatti without even campaigning there, and returned to Madras in February 1985 to take oath for the third time as chief minister.[8]

In the interim, Karunanidhi wrote in *Murasoli*, wishing his friend a speedy recovery, reminiscing about their days spent together as young wannabe cine workers.

But three years later, in the wee hours of 24 December 1987, the matinee idol succumbed to a cardiac arrest.

'Kalaignar had just reached Central station at 5 a.m. by train from either Erode or Coimbatore, I do not remember which,' says Duraimurugan. 'He was informed about MGR's death as soon as he arrived. He rushed straight to Ramavaram Gardens and garlanded his late friend, even before the announcement of his death was made.'

Duraimurugan recounts that it would have been impossible for Karunanidhi to have stayed by his friend's side in the mourning crowds. 'But only I was there with Kalaignar on the day MGR died. He was staying at a friend's house near Sivaji Ganesan's residence in T. Nagar. He cried all day for his friend. He never ate a morsel of food that day,' he says.

According to news reports at the time, over 4 million people arrived in Madras to pay homage to their leader, whose body was kept in state for twenty-nine hours before being buried near his mentor Annadurai's memorial on Marina Beach.

His wife, Janaki Ramachandran, was installed as the chief minister, with the party splintered over who should take charge of it.

But January of 1989 to January of 1991 was finally Karunanidhi's time, as he won the assembly polls. It was also the election that helped consolidate Jayalalithaa as the rightful political heir of MGR as her faction won twenty-seven seats as opposed to the Janaki faction which won only one. Janaki conceded defeat and the two factions of the party finally merged under the charismatic Jayalalithaa.

KARUNANIDHI AND JAYALALITHAA

If MGR and Karuna had a love–hate relationship, it was hatred from the word go between Karunanidhi and Jayalalithaa, especially on the latter's part.

'Jayalalithaa hated Kalaignar,' says Duraimurugan, who has watched the battles between both at close quarters. 'It began when MGR was still in the DMK and he asked Kalaignar to allow Jayalalithaa to speak at a Madurai rally of the DMK. Kalaignar said a firm no.'

In 1989, when it became clear that Jayalalithaa would take over MGR's mantle, Karunanidhi is said to have dismissed her as someone with no idea of Dravidian politics or ideology. Those close to him say that he mocked her, wondering how she could ever pose a challenge to him.

This was the second time in Karunanidhi's political career that he would severely underestimate an opponent. Jayalalithaa, despite being derided as an 'actress' and a 'Brahmin' (she was an Iyengar, the Vaishnavite sect of the Brahmin community) and 'not even Tamil' (she was born and raised in Mandya near Mysore in Karnataka), turned out to be a skilled administrator and a political tactician who honed what she had learnt from her mentor MGR as also from her bitterest foe Karunanidhi. On several occasions, she even outdid them.

It was an ugly event on 25 March 1989 when Karunanidhi and his DMK would find that Jayalalithaa was a force to reckon with. Karunanidhi, as chief minister, also held the finance portfolio and had begun to read out the budget speech. Jayalalithaa, in the Opposition, heckled him, continually interrupting him and preventing him from going ahead.

What happened next depends on whose version is taken into account. The DMK version is that Jayalalithaa screamed out, asking MLA Sengottaiyan to attack Karunanidhi. The AIADMK version is that DMK MLAs began to attack the Opposition.

Duraimurugan became infamous, subsequently, for allegedly yanking at and tearing Jayalalithaa's saree. In the melee that ensued, a weeping Jayalalithaa was bodily lifted by her party members and taken out to safety, her hair and clothes in disarray. Outside, to waiting media persons, Jayalalithaa swore that she would never set foot again in the Tamil Nadu assembly until it was a safe place for women. The episode, which had overtones of the Mahabharata and the disrobing of Draupadi by Duryodhana, brought a wave of sympathy for the young Jayalalithaa.[9]

'Nothing of the sort happened in the assembly,' argues Duraimurugan hotly. 'I have clarified this many times. It was a scene created by Thirunavukkarasar [then AIADMK MLA and, in 2018, president of the state unit of the Congress]. Moopanar [leader of the Tamil Maanila Congress and G.K. Vasan's father] was sitting next to Jayalalithaa in the assembly, right in front. I was at the back of the hall. Once the violence broke out, I came to the front and saw that Veerapandi Arumugam [DMK MLA] had a fountain of blood spurting from his forehead. K.K.S.S.R. Ramachandran [AIADMK MLA at the time and now a DMK leader] had hit him on the head with a microphone. I saw broken spectacles on the ground and picked them up as I escorted Arumugam to safety. I then went looking for my leader. He was sitting in another room, outside the assembly, and I stayed there with him. The broken spectacles were his. In fact, when this allegation of me misbehaving with Jayalalithaa was brought up later, Kalaignar said in public that if I had done such a thing then Karunanidhi would know, because I had been with him all along that day. Jayalalithaa was smart enough to make use of that situation.'

Irrespective of what the truth was, the people of Tamil Nadu chose to believe a wounded woman. Jayalalithaa also increasingly wooed the Congress under the leadership of Rajiv Gandhi as an ally, leaving the DMK out in the cold.

On 30 January 1991, Karunanidhi faced yet another setback. The Janata Dal (Secular) government, with Prime Minister Chandra Shekhar at the helm and backed by sixty MPs, largely of Rajiv Gandhi's Congress, dismissed the DMK government in Tamil Nadu.

The reason: having close ties with terrorist organizations like the LTTE of Sri Lanka. The daylight murder of Padmanabha, the chief of the rival EPRLF, in Madras, along with twelve of his party men and two innocent victims, triggered the furore. What made things much worse for Karunanidhi was that a minister in his cabinet, Subbulakshmi Jegadeesan, his own party workers and the state police were accused of aiding the murderers, members of the LTTE, to escape back to their country.

DMK leaders, including Duraimurugan, are mum about this period in the political history of the party. 'I know nothing about the LTTE,' says Duraimurugan firmly when queried on the subject.

Prime Minister Chandra Shekhar, egged on by ally Rajiv Gandhi, decided to crack down on the state government. The DMK government was dismissed. Four months later, Karunanidhi would find to his horror that the LTTE, whose cause of a separate Tamil Eelam in Sri Lanka he had enthusiastically supported, had struck again. On 21 May 1991, a young woman called Dhanu from the LTTE headed to Sriperumbudur to garland Rajiv Gandhi, who was campaigning for elections scheduled to be held a few days later. Strapped to her body was a bomb which exploded, killing the former prime minister, his assassin and fourteen others.

Tamil Nadu turned its back on Karunanidhi. Jayalalithaa, riding the sympathy wave for the slain Gandhi, an ally, ascended to the chief minister's post for the first time in May 1991.

But the truth, according to senior journalists in the state, is that Karunanidhi was only playing to the gallery on the issue of the Sri Lankan Tamils and the LTTE. 'There was no love lost between Kalaignar and the LTTE,' says N. Ram. 'He took it up as a rhetorical issue but it is well known that he was very angry and upset with the LTTE for killing Sri Sabaratnam [a Sri Lankan Tamil rebel and leader of the Tamil Eelam Liberation Organization]. In fact, he spoke to me at length on this. He said that he got information earlier that Sri Sabaratnam had been captured and was to be executed. So he called up "Baby" Subramaniam, who was quite close to Prabhakaran but had no decision-making authority. Kalaignar said he told him [Subramaniam] that Sri Sabaratnam was like his brother, closer than his brother, and he should not be executed. He was then shocked to learn that he had been tortured and killed.'

Prabhakaran was the leader of the LTTE, the armed rebel group that wanted a separate Eelam or state for Tamils in Sri Lanka. Sri Sabaratnam was the leader of the TELO (Tamil Eelam Liberation Organization), another group working towards the same cause. The LTTE and TELO did not see eye to eye on the issue of violence and suicide bombing of Sinhala leaders. 'Baby' Subramaniam was the head of the education division of the LTTE. Sabaratnam was killed in 1986 by the LTTE.

'When the war was going on, I said to Kalaignar when I met him, "Worse than a crime, a blunder." It is a quote wrongly attributed to Napoleon [Bonaparte],' continues Ram. 'The first blunder of the LTTE, I told him, was to take on the IPKF [Indian

Peace Keeping Force] for no good reason and then killing Rajiv Gandhi. The second blunder, I said, was to elect [Mahinda] Rajapaksa [in 2005]. He said, what do you mean? I said, yeah, they called for a boycott in the Tamil areas in an extremely close presidential poll because they did not want Ranil Wickremasinghe to win. [But Rajapaksa, who won the election, would eventually intensify the war against the LTTE, culminating in Prabhakaran's death in 2009.] Then he said one more blunder the LTTE made was to kill Sri Sabaratnam in a horrible way – torturing and killing him – even though he [Karunanidhi] had interceded. He was very critical of the LTTE.

'Kalaignar was very moderate. He spoke up for the Tamils. When the Indian emissaries went, he demanded a ceasefire but he didn't make it impossible for the Centre to conduct its political diplomacy,' explains Ram.

From 1991 to 1996, Karunanidhi and the DMK watched as Jayalalithaa, along with her close aide and confidante Sasikala Natarajan (as she was then known; now she prefers to be called V.K. Sasikala), ruled over the state. Announcing after she came to power that the DMK had emptied the treasury and that she would take only a token Re 1 salary as chief minister, Jayalalithaa began work on a slew of welfare schemes targeted at the woman voter.

Political thuggery too was at an all-time high as vengeance was wreaked upon DMK members for various slights, both real and perceived. Jayalalithaa brought on her own downfall in 1995 in the form of a jaw-dropper of a wedding for her foster son V.N. Sudhakaran, a nephew of Sasikala's, to the granddaughter of cine actor Sivaji Ganesan.

The pomp and show put on in Madras for the wedding disgusted the voters. As the *New York Times*'s John F. Burns wrote in astonishment on 10 September 1995:

> Brushing aside court challenges from opponents who accused her of turning large parts of the city into a private theme park, she deployed thousands of state workers for weeks preparing a specially built, cardboard and papier-mache 'fort' that covered an area as big as several football fields near the Indian Ocean waterfront. At least 12,000 of the guests sat down to a wedding lunch, served by 3,500 cooks and waiters.[10]

The report further stated that one of India's leading film-set designers was summoned to make whole avenues in central Madras into a tableau of Tamil mythology. For miles between Jayalalithaa's official residence and the wedding site, streets were decorated with pillared castles decorated with Grecian statues and gilded lions. Shrines were erected, with icon-like images of Jayalalithaa in place of Hindu gods.

The report went on to say, 'With scores of tumbling acrobats, regiments of mounted horsemen, hundreds of truckload of flowers, at least 20,000 policemen on special duty, and invitations to thousands of guests inscribed on silver salvers, it was not an event to be financed on a politician's salary. Ms. Jayalalitha, entitled to a Chief Minister's pay of $330 a month, has said that she draws only one rupee monthly, equivalent to about three American cents.'

In 1996, voters turned their back on her. Karunanidhi was again in the seat of power. He then initiated a series of corruption cases against Jayalalithaa. One such case was the colour TV scam, wherein colour TV sets were allegedly bought at prices higher than the market price, with the Jayalalithaa government allegedly making Rs 10.16 crore in the deal. On 7 December 1998, Jayalalithaa, Sasikala and seven others of the AIADMK were jailed for thirty days as hearings continued. During this period, her residence in Poes Garden, Chennai, was raided and the DMK's propaganda channel, Sun TV, streamed live visuals of 30 kg of gold, including 400 bangles, over 100 wrist watches, 10,000 sarees and hundreds of pairs of footwear, amongst other dizzyingly expensive possessions.[11]

It was also during the initial days of the Karunanidhi government that a Disproportionate Assets case was slapped on Jayalalithaa, Sasikala, Sasikala's sister-in-law Ilavarasi and nephew V.N. Sudhakaran. This case would go on for close to two decades, ending in a 'guilty' verdict finally after Jayalalithaa's death in 2016, putting Sasikala and the others behind bars for four years.

After the dust settled on the cases and the DMK government went about in earnest wooing industry to Tamil Nadu and focusing on development of the state, the people of Tamil Nadu, in 2001, once again did an about-turn. To Jayalalithaa's aid came a shimmering alliance: the Tamil Maanila Congress, the Left parties, the Congress and the Pattali Makkal Katchi, along with a smattering of smaller parties, did the trick for the AIADMK. The DMK, in alliance with the BJP, found itself deserted by every party with any standing in the state.

So much so that Karunanidhi, who was confident of being re-elected, was bitter when the results were announced. *Frontline* magazine recorded at the time: 'Karunanidhi's gamble that people would vote the DMK again to power on the strength of its government's impressive performance proved wrong. Voters everywhere appreciated his government's performance but this did not translate to votes. The hurt on this score showed when Karunanidhi sarcastically said, "I consider the verdict a gift from the people of Tamil Nadu for the successive achievements of our rule in the past five years."'[12]

It was again time for vendetta. By midnight on 29 June 2001, Sun TV's camera crew was in place on Oliver Road in Mylapore,

Karunanidhi's second residence. Just after midnight, a posse of policemen descended to arrest the Opposition leader on a case relating to public money being allegedly siphoned off in the building of flyovers in Chennai. Around 1.30 a.m., police moved in, broke open the bedroom door and dragged the ageing leader out, as Sun TV beamed these visuals live across the state. Visuals showed Karunanidhi falling, being shoved, picked up and pushed again by the police, evoking a wave of sympathy for the elderly man.

Two Union ministers, T.R. Baalu and Murasoli Maran, too were arrested. The BJP-led NDA government at the Centre, of which the DMK was an ally, was forced to intervene. Following pressure from the Centre, Jayalalithaa had no choice but to backtrack in the face of calls of 'Constitutional breakdown' in the state. First, the Union ministers were let off, the charges against them dropped. Karunanidhi was then allowed out on bail on 'humanitarian grounds'.[13] Jayalalithaa had had her revenge. But Karunanidhi won the war.

Jayalalithaa went on to press her self-destruct button yet again as her tenure continued. In July 2003, she invoked the ESMA (Essential Services Maintenance Act) on one lakh striking government employees, terminating their employment. Realizing her monumental error, she reinstated them all in February 2004. In 2003, she also banned animal sacrifice, once again causing widespread indignation and protests across the state. A few months later, she repealed the Act. But the damage was done.

By 2006, the DMK had cobbled up a rainbow alliance ahead of the assembly polls. Despite the niggling resentment against Jayalalithaa for her earlier moves, the election was largely without a major issue or talking point. But the genius politician in Karunanidhi struck. Free colour televisions for all those below the poverty line, he promised. Tamil Nadu brought him back to power as Jayalalithaa watched. And learned.

The tenure from 2006 to 2011 was the undoing of Karunanidhi, as elaborated in the earlier chapters. Governance took a back seat. Jayalalithaa simply had to sit by and watch as Karunanidhi and his family and party men and women destroyed their own credibility and popularity in the state.

In 2011, an alliance with 'Captain' Vijaykanth, a bright new player in the political arena, was locked in by Jayalalithaa. She swept the state as people vented their anger against the excesses of the DMK in the past five years.

Despite little to no governance between 2011 and 2016, cash for votes played a huge role in 2016. The memories of the DMK's muscling and land grabbing still fresh in their minds, Tamil Nadu voters brought Jayalalithaa back to power, albeit with a slimmer majority.

Here on, age would catch up with the veteran politician. In 2016, he was hospitalized a number of times. He lost his ability to speak as a tracheostomy tube was put in place. But his love for politics, power and the people still remains.

Duraimurugan recounts an incident from November 2017, when he watched his leader undergo speech therapy. The tracheostomy tube was removed, the hole in the throat closed with a finger and speech therapist Ranjith began.

'"What is your name?" he asked Kalaignar. "En peyar Mu Karunanidhi," he answered,' says Duraimurugan, mimicking his leader's raspy voice perfectly. (My name is M. Karunanidhi.)

'"Ranjith: Who do you like?"

"Kalaignar: Arignar Anna."

"Anna is a name that occupies his mind," he concluded.'

Duraimurugan recounts another incident from the next day, when Karunanidhi began to question Ranjith:

'"Kalaignar: How is my voice?"

"Ranjith: Your voice is good, Ayya."

"Kalaignar: Do you think people can understand me if I speak at meetings?"'

With that, Duraimurugan simply shakes his head. 'What can you say about someone like that?' he smiles.

6

CASES AND CONTROVERSIES

The first blot on Karunanidhi's sparkling political career came in the form of MGR's allegations of mismanagement of party funds in 1972. In November that year, MGR went a step further after being unceremoniously expelled from the DMK. He, along with his loyalists, sent memorandums to the President of India, asking for a Commission of Inquiry to be set up to probe corruption charges against then Chief Minister M. Karunanidhi.

> Shri M. Kalyanasundaram, M.P., and five others viz S/Shri K. Baladhandayudham, M.P., K.T.K. Thangamani, M.L.A., K.T. Raju, P. Manickam, M.V. Sundaram and S. Narayanan, all of the Communist Party of India, submitted a Memorandum, dated November 6, 1972, to the President of India, making similar allegations chiefly against Shri M. Karunanidhi and his companion Ministers of the D.M.K. Government.[1]

The R.S. Sarkaria Commission looked into a large number of allegations of corruption made by MGR, his loyalists and the CPI. Below is a gist of the allegations made and the details of the various scams.

1) **The Nathan Press Scandal:** A key minister in Karunanidhi's cabinet, Anbil Dharmalingam, was one of the many ministers named in the corruption allegations probed by the Sarkaria Commission. The commission's first report details how Nathan Press, which was owned by Pandurangam and Kasturi Chettiar in Trichy, was in fact a benami for Dharmalingam. In 1968, shortly after the DMK first came to power, a new enterprise, Nathan Publications, was begun, with Dharmalingam's sister Dhanamanickam as a partner along with Pandurangam and others. Two years later, the Tamil Nadu Textbook Society was formed and Nathan Publications got a plum contract for printing and distribution of textbooks despite quoting a higher rate in the bids. The report details how Nathan Publications got more and more business from the government in the ensuing years, despite having no prior experience in printing textbooks, a basic prerequisite to even participate in the bids. In enabling Dharmalingam to obtain these contracts for Nathan Publications, Minister V.R. Nedunchezhiyan was a keen facilitator.

Year[2]	Percentage of Commission	Total Commission Allowed (Rs)
1970-71	6	18,496.55
	7	16,106.12
1971-72	6	24,781.89
	7	20,364.58
1972-73	10	1,80,821.32

1973-74	10	1,18,084.90
1974-75	10	1,39,817.11
1975-76 (up to 31-1-76)	12	1,82,716.08
Total		**Rs 7,01,188.55**

The table here shows that (a) the percentage of commission paid by the government to Nathan Press for printing textbooks was higher than that for other vendors and (b) the number of contracts given to Nathan Press increased over the years.

Let us look at some more examples of corruption in the Karunanidhi government, as detailed in the Sarkaria Commission's first report.

2) **Aerial Spraying of Crops:** When the Centre, under Prime Minister Indira Gandhi introduced a subsidized scheme for state governments to aerially spray pesticides on crops, Agriculture Minister Anbil Dharmalingam once again made a killing, through another benami firm called Ponni Enterprises. This was also one of the more serious charges against Karunanidhi directly as the aviation companies that won the tenders for aerial spraying deposed in detail before the Commission about how the chief minister's private secretary, IAS officer Vaithialingam, entered the scene and demanded large sums in return for getting the contracts. The contracts were subsequently inflated and the Commission showed how both Dharmalingam, his friends and Karunanidhi made a sizeable amount under the table.

The Commission observed in its report: 'Vaithialingam, CW6, the then Private Secretary to the Chief Minister, Shri M. Karunanidhi, appears to have come forward with a full disclosure of all the relevant facts within his knowledge concerning the demand, collection or receipt of this gratification or commission. He has testified how through him, Shri Karunanidhi conveyed instructions to coerce the Operators to pay gratification to him and how he was instructed to induce H.P. Rao to pay a gratification of Rs 25,000 to the Chief Minister, through him on 17th November 1970, as a consideration for allotting him aerial spraying work at the rate of Rs 9 per acre for an acreage of 1.5 lakhs. He has further deposed how under his advice, H.P. Rao paid through the witness on 13th August 1971, another sum of Rs 25,000 to the Chief Minister and how immediately thereupon, instructions from the Chief Minister for immediate payment of the bills of Pushpaka Aviation and delivery of the signed contract deed to that concern were communicated to the Director of Agriculture and the Secretary, Agriculture. He has also deposed to the meetings of the Operators with him on 19th September 1971 and again on 20th September 1971 and his communicating to the Operators the desire of the Chief Minister that the Operators should pay 90 paise per acre as commission, in advance, for the acreages covered up to the 19th September 1971, and how after discussion the Operators agreed to pay the same in two equal instalments calculated at 45 paise per acre, and how in compliance with this demand, Cambata and Captain made to the witness, on 22nd September 1971, the collective payment of Rs 1,17,273 which was immediately thereafter passed on by the witness to the Chief Minister, Shri Karunanidhi, at the latter's residence.'[3]

What is extraordinary in this case is not just the frank deposition of Karunanidhi's private secretary and his admission of having actively aided corruption and

An undated photo of a young Karunanidhi.

All photos in this section have
from The Hindu Archives.

With mentor and then chief minister C.N. Annadurai in Madras in September 1967. Karunanidhi was public works minister in his cabinet at the time.

With M.G. Ramachandran, a friend he brought into politics who later became his nemesis, at the Madras airport in July 1970.
Photo: S. Kothandaraman

Handing over a gift for the jawans fighting the India-Pakistan war to Prime Minister Indira Gandhi in New Delhi in 1971. Karunanidhi had been her key supporter in the dramatic presidential election of 1969 but later turned a bitter opponent of the Emergency imposed by her.

With Prime Minister Rajiv Gandhi at the Madras airport in 1989. Under the DMK, the LTTE had a free run in Tamil Nadu, resulting in Gandhi's assasination two years later.

The DMK under Karunanidhi was a crucial ally at the Centre in a number of governments. Here he is seen with Prime Minister P.V. Narasimha Rao in New Delhi in May 1996.

With Prime Minister Atal Bihari Vajpayee in New Delhi in April 1998. When he refused to give in to Jayalalithaa's demand for the dismissal of Karunanidhi's government in 1999, she withdrew her support at the Centre and Vajpayee lost the no-confidence motion in Parliament by a single vote.

Sitting in front of the Central Jail in Chennai the night after Chief Minister J. Jayalalithaa infamously had the police drag him out of his home at midnight in June 2001 for his alleged involvement in a scam related to the construction of flyovers in the city.
Photo: R. Ragu

M.K. Stalin, seen here with his father in 2004, was appointed the working president of the DMK in 2017 after Karunanidhi's health declined and is seen as the one most likely to succeed him. Photo: V. Ganesan

Calling on then Congress president and UPA chairperson Sonia Gandhi at her residence in New Delhi in June 2006. The DMK was an important constituent of UPA I and II from 2004 to 2014, and Karunanidhi often professed respect and admiration for Gandhi. Photo: R.V. Moorthy

Of his six children, Karunanidhi is said to have a soft spot for his daughter Kanimozhi, seen here at the inauguration of a cultural festival with him in Chennai in January 2013. She is also the only one who calls a spade a spade to the larger-than-life leader.
Photo: R. Shivaji Rao

Tamil Nadu has a history of personalities from the film fraternity entering politics. The list, which includes Karunanidhi himself, now also has Kamal Haasan and Rajinikanth, the two stars seen here at a film premiere in Chennai in July 2008 with the ageing leader.
Photo: M. Vedhan

collection of commission, but also that the initial minister for agriculture before Dharmalingam – Sathyavani Muthu – had refused to entertain higher rates for aerial spraying. This decision had been struck down unilaterally by Karunanidhi and she was asked to sign on a rate pre-determined by him. Muthu gave a frank and damning account of what took place, indicting Karunanidhi in the charges of corruption against him.

'This circumstance definitely points to the conclusion that both Shri Karunanidhi and Shri Anbil Dharmalingam were acting in concert in squeezing out these gratifications in the shape of the commission from the Operators,' said the Commission's first report, while stating that bribes worth Rs 1,42,273 were collected by Vaithialingam on behalf of Karunanidhi, while Dharmalingam collected a sum of Rs 3,87,746 from the aviation firms.

The state government, predictably, went all out to protect its leader. Law Minister Madhavan, a close aide of Karunanidhi's, was accused by the CBI of keeping in his possession a file that contained incriminating documents. State government departments did not allow the CBI to inspect or take into their possession any files or documents, despite repeated requests. The CBI wrote to the Commission, stating that either documents were not made available or that incomplete documents were allowed to be inspected by the CBI.

3) **Land for New Globe Theatre:** In 1938, one Varadaraja Pillai took 11 ¾ grounds of land on Mount Road in Madras on lease for a period of fifteen years and three months. He had built a cinema theatre called the New Globe Theatre and the lease was extended for another ten years upon expiry

of the original lease period. The owners, according to the original agreement, had the option of buying the land and the building back for a sum of Rs 50,000. When they tried to do so, Pillai refused to hand over the property and the case went all the way to the Supreme Court. The owners won the case and Pillai was to hand over the land and the building to the owners by 17 February 1972, according to the judgement. This did not happen, and Pillai instead approached various courts in order to hold on to the land. Finally, having exhausted all his options and lost all his appeals, Pillai gave up the land and building to the owners on 24 March 1974. He died on 21 May 1974.

Pillai's son, Sivaramasubramanian, deposed before the Commission that when his father was admitted in a nursing home in Madras in November 1971, he had asked him to go home and pick up Rs 30,000 kept in a safe and hand it over to Karunanidhi at his Gopalapuram residence. The report based on the deposition says, 'The witness [Sivaramasubramanian] found the amount of Rs 30,000 in a brown cover in the safe of his house. He took that cover containing the money to the Chief Minister's house in Gopalapuram at about 8 p.m. He sent a slip bearing his name and that of his father through a peon to the Chief Minister who was sitting alone in a room upstairs. The witness was then called upstairs and the peon ushered the witness into that room. The Chief Minister received the cover and said "Sari" [all right]. The Chief Minister did not, in the presence of the witness, examine the contents of the cover, or check-up the currency notes. After handing over the money, the witness returned to the nursing home and reported compliance to his father.

'Sivasubramanian further stated that in February 1972, the Madras City Tenants' Protection Act was amended...

which was passed by the State Legislature in about two months' time, after the payment of the money to the Chief Minister.' Using this amendment, Pillai filed a review petition in the Madras High Court, which was dismissed, and later in the Supreme Court, which too dismissed it.

Other witnesses in this case speak of how Pillai paid Rs 40,000 to then Revenue Minister P.U. Shanmugam in order to get the relevant law amended. Shanmugam directed Pillai and his friends to meet the chief minister. One witness deposed that Pillai had told him that he had met Karunanidhi through MP Murasoli Maran and that the chief minister had demanded a bribe of Rs 60,000 since Rs 40,000 had already been paid to Shanmugam. Pillai is said to have told this witness that he had pleaded with the chief minister that he could only afford another Rs 30,000 and he had agreed.

During the hearings of the Sarkaria Commission, it became abundantly clear that various ministers had brought pressure upon bureaucrats to amend the legislation, despite their stating that it was not good in law. Here is an excerpt:

> Shri V. Sundaram, Collector, Tirunelveli District, who had dealt with this case as Deputy Secretary, Revenue, has deposed in para 21 of his affidavit: 'Extra administrative *and undue pressure* was brought to bear upon me by the then Minister for Food and Revenue Shri P.U. Shanmugham and the Personal Assistant to the Minister, Shri Kuppuswamy. He stated that after he had recorded the note to the effect that there was no case to amend the Tamil Nadu City Tenants' Protection Act, 1922, he was personally requested by both the

> Minister for Food and Revenue and his Personal Assistant to reconsider my view. The Minister for Food and Revenue Shri P.U. Shanmugham told me. The Deputy Secretary states that he had: Firmly indicated time and again to both the Minister and his Personal Assistant that as a public servant I reserved the right to tender impartial and fearless advice to the Government which could always take a final decision in the matter.
>
> About half a dozen MLAs of the then ruling Party had also contacted the Deputy Secretary twice or thrice, every day during the period from 20th November 1971 to 10th December 1971, with a view to pressurize him to change his views. He distinctly remembers Shri Vezhavendan, a prominent leader of the Ruling Party, leading a deputation of MLAs in order to persuade him to put up a favourable note. After his firm refusal to accede to the request of the MLAs, the Deputy Secretary adds, the Minister for Food and Revenue (Shri P.U. Shanmugham) 'called me to his room for the second time and expressed his dissatisfaction that I was not prepared to change my mind in the matter. Even then, I declined the suggestion of the Minister for Food & Revenue.'

The amendment to the legislation too was carried out in a hurry, breaking the rule that an amendment being introduced to the House must be given at least three days' time for the other members to read through and critique. The amendment, in this case, was given to other members only the previous day before the Bill was introduced. Also, in order to get the necessary approvals from the Centre and the President of India, bureaucrats in fact travelled 'by air', a rare proposition in those years, to Delhi.

Justice Sarkaria summed this case up with an interesting observation. He stated that while it was clear that Karunanidhi, Law Minister Madhavan and Food and Revenue Minister P.U. Shanmugam were motivated to push the amendment through in a rush in order to help Pillai, whether they received monetary benefit for the same was not proven.

4) **'Generosity' to A.L. Srinivasan of Sarada Studios:** When prohibition was lifted by Karunanidhi in 1971, the field was thrown open to industrialists who wanted to manufacture and retail liquor. Accordingly, bids were invited from interested industrialists to apply for the same. Thirty applications were received by the government, according to the Sarkaria Commission report. For beer production alone, the chief minister appears to have stepped in and shortlisted eight names. Of these, A.L. Srinivasan is one. Strangely, Srinivasan had not even applied for a licence for beer production and his name was not among the list of thirty applicants.

Srinivasan submitted an application two weeks after the list was drawn up, and got the licence – despite being insolvent, not even having a piece of land, and continually asking for extensions to fulfil the licence conditions. Finally, he never got to set up the brewery as prohibition was re-imposed in 1974.

5) **A Murder and a Saviour:** On 6 April 1971, in Jangamarajapuram hamlet in Anbil village, Trichy district, home to minister Dharmalingam, a murder took place.

Around 8.15 p.m., one Manickam was lying down outside his house, when four people arrived with sticks and spears and murdered him.

The four accused were: A1 – Karutha Babu, brother of Ayeepillai; A2 – Palaniandi Sholagar, father-in-law of Dharmalingam; A3 – Veerayyan, co-brother of Palaniandi Sholagar; and A4 – Ayeepillai, mother-in-law of Dharmalingam.

With the intervention of the village munsiff, the local police and the district administration, it was quickly decided that only Karutha Babu would face the music. The other three, closely related to the minister, were removed from the list of accused.

On 29 January 1972, the sessions judge of Trichy acquitted the sole accused, Karutha Babu, while passing strictures against the police and the prosecution: 'He [the Police Officer] has registered the case against the accused and 3 other persons mentioned in the report Exhibit P-l. But unfortunately, the Police Officer who investigated the case has chosen to lay the chargesheet only against the accused for reasons best known to himself...The Police Officer in this case has taken the role of a Judge...The prosecution has not examined any other person in the locality.'

In effect, proximity to the minister had ensured that four people involved in a murder had got away scot-free. Since there was no firm evidence on record to show that the minister or his cabinet colleagues had interfered in order to 'collapse' the prosecution's case, the Commission simply observed that the officials concerned had acted with the knowledge that the accused were related to the minister.

6) **The Sugar Scandal:** The accusation by MGR on this issue read thus: 'The Chief Minister got the rights for releasing of sugar bags from private sugar mills. The Chief Minister and Food Minister, P.U. Shanmugam, demanded Rs 2 to Rs 3 per bag of sugar released and collected a sum estimated at over Rs 50 lakhs, through a leading Flour Mill Industrialist of Madras. Much to the dislike of the Chief Minister, Messrs Parry & Co. Ltd, under the Chairmanship of Mr H.V.R. Iyengar, Ex-Governor of Reserve Bank of India, resisted initially the payment of Rs 2 to Rs 3 per bag and the ensuing struggle resulted in the exit of an able Chairman, since about Rs 100 lakhs worth of sugar bags got accumulated in godowns, for want of release orders for which hush money was not forthcoming from them.'

In 1969-70, India witnessed an unprecedented production of sugar – 42 lakh tonne. As supply surged, prices dropped. This meant that the prices of 'levy sugar' or PDS sugar and 'free sugar' or sugar sold in the free market were almost the same. It was a problem of too much, as Tamil Nadu's sugar mills were unable to store the excess sugar produced and they pleaded with the government to allow them to sell the sugar out. Only if the sugar was bought could cane growers, mill owners and the entire chain of sugar producers be paid.

The Madras branch of the South India Sugar Mills Association (SISMA) approached then Food Minister Shanmugam, asking for the government to resolve the issue. Their request was to allow the mill owners to sell the excess sugar directly to wholesalers since the government was not buying it. The minister said he would consult the chief minister.

The chief minister, at a meeting with the SISMA members, reportedly demanded a bribe of Rs 3 per bag of sugar. The other condition was that all mill owners should be onboard. If even one of them dissented, there was no deal.

But the chairman of EID Parry, H.V.R. Iyengar, refused to fall in line with the rest of the mill owners who had reluctantly agreed to the deal. The Sarkaria Commission Report records his testimony: 'I put my foot down and said that Parry had a long and unsullied reputation and I was not going to countenance any clandestine payment, however grim the situation in the Companies in the Group. Corruption is always bad, but to bleed an industry which was in the doldrums was, to my mind, most reprehensible.'

Pressure was brought on Iyengar by other members of the association and he then agreed. In February 1970, Minister Shanmugam passed the requisite order.

An amount of Rs 3.77 lakh was collected by the mills at the rate of Rs 3 per bag. Upon further pleading with the chief minister to reduce the exorbitant bribe amount, he acquiesced and halved the rate. In the next round, the sugar mills collected Rs 97,000 at the rate of Rs 1.50 per bag. The third instalment was of the order of Rs 91,818 and the fourth instalment of Rs 81,516. The bribes continued to flow along with the sugar. A total of sixteen payments were allegedly made to Karunanidhi by the SISMA. In 1971, sugar was finally decontrolled and, with it, the kickbacks came to an end.

The Commission concluded that Karunanidhi and Shanmugam had indeed taken the illegal gratifications amounting to Rs 13 lakh and thus helped sugar mill owners make money by depriving government coffers of a similar amount.

7) **The Veeranam Project:** In case of the Veeranam project in Cuddalore, the Commission stated that while there was

no evidence to prove that Karunanidhi indeed took bribes from a contractor, the responsibility for losses of crores of rupees to the exchequer rested squarely on his shoulders.

This allegation was based on the Veeranam drinking water project handed over to the Sathyanarayana brothers, who had no experience in that field. The project was awarded to them after Karunanidhi personally instructed officials to tailor-make the conditions for the project so as to suit the brothers.

One of them, Purushotthaman, was a close friend of Murasoli Maran and had built the Murasoli building for him free of charge. The allegation of payment of Rs 29 lakh by Purushotthaman to the chief minister was not established. The brothers were then given lavish advances by the government towards the project, which remained incomplete for years.

The accountant general is reported to have pointed out that the state had lost Rs 6 crore over this project. 'To the public exchequer, it would mean an additional burden of several crores, and to the public looking long for adequate water supply, a tortuous wait for at least two years more. The responsibility for this huge waste of public money must rest squarely on Shri Karunanidhi…' said the Commission.

When the interim report of the Sarkaria Commission was 'leaked' to the press on 16 February 1977, it provided MGR and his cohorts much glee. Justice Sarkaria stated in that report that the evidence against Karunanidhi and the ministers was 'cogent, convincing and reliable'.[4]

But the final report of the Sarkaria Commission, placed before the Rajya Sabha on 2 March 1977, turned out to be a huge disappointment for MGR. Karunanidhi had been given a clean chit – well, almost. The Commission failed to find any evidence to pin the then chief minister down on any of the allegations against him, except for the aerial spraying scam and the sugar scandal. Even these could not be actionable, despite MGR's best efforts.

'The mystery in this issue is the extraordinary money power of Karunanidhi and how it has made many clinching witnesses turn hostile,' says C. Ponnaiyan, finance minister in MGR's regime and one of the petitioners along with him to have precipitated the Sarkaria Commission.

'When Karunanidhi and team requested Morarji Desai [prime minister from 1977 to 1979], he refused to interfere in judicial administration. But subsequently Karunanidhi very trickily made use of the political situation in our country. He was able to wriggle out of strong evidence-based cases,' says Ponnaiyan.

In the words of Justice Sarkaria, allegedly uttered during one of the hearings and famously repeated incessantly by AIADMK leaders, 'scientific corruption' had allowed the wily politician to get away with barely a scratch.

THE JAIN COMMISSION

As the Sarkaria Commission furore died down, MGR came to power in 1977 and his government was dissolved briefly between February and June 1980. But he returned to helm the state, battling crippling illness, and remained in power until 1987, when he breathed his last. The succession struggle that erupted within the AIADMK after MGR's passing helped the DMK come to power briefly between 1989 and 1991.

The government, though, was dissolved once again and President's Rule imposed between 30 January and 24 June 1991. The reason: the DMK and Karunanidhi's alleged support for the

LTTE in Sri Lanka in their separatist cause for a Tamil nation. What made matters worse for Karunanidhi was that former Prime Minister Rajiv Gandhi was assassinated by a suicide bomber on Tamil Nadu soil, in Sriperumbudur on 21 May 1991, as he was campaigning for elections. Dhanu, a member of the LTTE, blew herself up along with Gandhi as she garlanded him at a public rally. A manhunt was launched for other members of the hit team that was on the run.

Karunanidhi was shell-shocked. 'He probably never imagined that Prabhakaran and the LTTE would do such a thing,' says N. Ram.

The Jain Commission was then set up, and Karunanidhi found himself once again in the crosshairs of a probe that could finish him. The Jain Commission of Inquiry was a successor to the Justice J.S. Verma Commission, which looked into one set of aspects of the Rajiv Gandhi assassination. However, with the bereaved Congress clamouring for a widening of the scope of the inquiry, retired Justice M.C. Jain was asked to probe other aspects of the case.

In August 1991, the Commission was born and its mandate was as follows:

2. The commission shall make an inquiry with respect to the following matters:

a) the sequence of events leading to and all the facts and circumstances relating to the assassination of Shri Rajiv Gandhi at Sriperumbudur (other than the matters covered by the terms of reference for the Commission of Inquiry headed by Shri Justice J.S Verma);

b) whether any person or persons or agencies were responsible for conceiving, preparing and planning the assassination and whether there was any conspiracy in this behalf and, if so, all its ramifications...

4. The Commission may, if it deems fit, make interim reports to the Central Government before the said date on any of the matters mentioned in paragraph 2 above.[5]

The interim report of the Jain Commission, tabled before Parliament in August 1997, goes into details of the history of the struggle for Tamil rights in the Sinhala-dominant island nation and the subsequent militancy that ensued. A brief account of the history is needed at this juncture for the reader to understand the prevailing mood at the time.

In his deposition before the Jain Commission in November 1996, Karunanidhi himself gave a description of how close the ties between the Tamils of Tamil Nadu and those of Sri Lanka were: 'India and Sri Lanka are geographically very closely located. Prior to Independence, during the British rule, the Collector of Thanjavur was administering the affairs of the Sri Lanka's Jaffna District/peninsula. The distance between India and Sri Lanka is so small that if one stands in Kodikarai, Point Calimere of Thanjavur, he can see the lights of Kankesanthurai in Jaffna. The distance between India and Sri Lanka is within about 20 km,' he stated.[6]

Sri Lanka too was a British colony and Tamils, with their knowledge of English, came to be favoured over the Sinhalese in government jobs. This led to resentment towards the Tamils in the majority Sinhalese population – 70 per cent of the populace. As a result, Sinhala hardliners emerged, demanding that the Tamils be sidelined. Pogroms began, becoming commonplace from 1956 onwards. Sinhala leaders began to openly attack the Tamils of northern Sri Lanka.

One of the first voices of protest against the discrimination of Tamils was that of S.J.V. Chelvanayagam, who belonged to the Federal Party. Chelvanayagam's was a non-violent voice and peace agreements were signed between him, his successors and the Sinhalese government 1957 onwards. None of the agreements were, however, enforced.

The unrest continued well into the 1970s, with the displacement of lakhs of Tamils, violence in the northern countryside, the burning of the beautiful Jaffna library and other oppressive measures. In 1972, Velupillai Prabhakaran began an organization called the TNT, the Tamil New Tigers. Born into a fisherman caste with a father of Malaysian-Tamil origin, Prabhakaran was, according to the interim Jain Commission report, 'deeply traumatized by seeing one of his uncles burnt alive during the language riots of 1958. Prabhakaran gradually emerged as a fascist militant leader with a cult of personality in the militant movement.'[7]

The TNT organized armed attacks – one main victim was the mayor of Jaffna. They also looted banks. In May 1976, Prabhakaran founded the LTTE. So much did violence and conflict intensify that, by 1978, the Sri Lankan government banned the LTTE and other Tamil militant groups.

Eelam Revolutionary Organization of Students or Eelam Revolutionary Organizers (EROS) was started by a Sri Lankan Tamil, Eliyathamby Ratnasabapathy, who lived in Britain. When in 1976 they opened a military training camp in Vavuniya, Sri Lanka, Prabhakaran was among the first to be trained there. EROS built close connections with and received training from armed rebel groups in Palestine, such as the Palestine Liberation Organization (PLO). EROS's student wing, called the General Union of Eelam Students, was formed in Madras.

A faction led by K. Padmanabha broke from the EROS and formed the EPRLF – the Eelam People's Revolutionary Liberation Front. In 1990, Padmanabha, twelve of his men and two bystanders were murdered in broad daylight in Madras's

Kodambakkam area. Two armed men, both members of the LTTE, arrived in a stolen Ambassador car and gunned down the thirteen members of the EPRLF who were holding a meeting. This daring murder and the delayed reaction of the state government under Chief Minister Karunanidhi, which allowed the murderers to escape to Sri Lanka, were among the main causes for the DMK government to be dissolved in 1991.

The home secretary of the state, R. Nagarajan, and Subbulakshmi Jegadeesan, then a minister in the Karunanidhi cabinet, were named as accused. The draconian TADA – Terrorist and Disruptive Activities (Prevention) Act – was slapped on them along with fifteen others. A special TADA court in Poonamallee tried them. Allegations against the home secretary were that he had instructed the police not to act against the murderers. The charge against Subbulakshmi Jegadeesan and her husband was that they had housed one of the murderers, Gundu Santhan. But charges against them were quashed for lack of evidence. Only two of the seventeen accused were convicted and sent to prison.

The Tamil Eelam Liberation Organization (TELO) was another important pro-Tamil outfit in the island nation. It was founded in 1979 by Thangadorai and Kuttimani and was involved in robbing banks. After the arrest of the founders, Sri Sabaratnam took over as its leader in 1981. Karunanidhi and Sri Sabaratnam were close friends and shared mutual respect. When Sri Sabaratnam was kidnapped by the LTTE, Karunanidhi is said to have passed on a message to Prabhakaran asking that the man's life be spared. To his shock, the LTTE tortured and killed him in a most brutal fashion.

The interim report records how tensions intensified in the 1980s: 'In the wake of 1980s, the situation prevailing in Sri Lanka was delicate. Tamil militancy had gained ground in Sri Lanka. Some prominent Tamil militant leaders, notably, V. Prabhakaran of the LTTE, had started frequently visiting Tamil Nadu and staying there for considerable length of time. These militant groups had begun establishing bases in Tamil Nadu. The Sri Lankan Government's repeated crackdown on the Tamil militants and the frequent anti-Tamil riots had led to large number of Sri Lankan Tamil refugees fleeing the island to the proximate Eastern coast of Tamil Nadu,' read the report.[8] Tamil nationalism, the perceived umbilical bond with the Tamils of Sri Lanka and a sympathetic political leadership allowed the militants a safe haven in the state.

Justice Jain crucified Karunanidhi in his interim report. When IPKF men were sent to Sri Lanka as part of the Indo-Sri Lanka Accord of 1987, accusations were rife that they were targeting the Tamils and that there were rapes and murders aplenty by the Indian armed forces: 'They [the LTTE] sent personal emissaries to Karunanidhi for seeking his active support in their battle against the Indian Peace Keeping Force (IPKF) ... These overtures of the LTTE towards the DMK started a chain of events which led to LTTE's survival and growth in Tamil Nadu even after the attitude of the Government of India had changed towards the LTTE after the hostilities between the IPKF and LTTE in Sri Lanka,' stated the report.[9]

Jain also noted that the LTTE was getting 'supplies, including arms, ammunition, explosives, fuel and other essential items for its war against the IPKF from Tamil Nadu. That too with the support of the Tamil Nadu government and the connivance of the law enforcement authorities ... LTTE activities of arms smuggling, abduction of Indian citizens and officials and intimidation of the law enforcement machinery were tolerated' by the DMK government, it said.[10]

The interim report caused a furore when it was presented to then Home Minister Indrajit Gupta on 28 August 1997. *India Today* magazine reported that the '5,280-page report, comprising eight volumes of interim findings and nine volumes of annexures bound in black rexine, holds Tamil Nadu Chief Minister M. Karunanidhi and his DMK responsible for abetting Rajiv Gandhi's murderers. Also blamed are two former prime ministers, V.P. Singh and Chandra Shekhar, for their laxity in assessing the threat to Rajiv.'[11]

Karunanidhi's protests of innocence were waved away. In a deposition before the Commission in January 1997, he said: 'I had supported the LTTE along with other parties, but after the murder of Padmanabha, I withdrew my support.' This statement, though, was not accepted by Jain.

The United Front government fell as its ally, the DMK, was accused of facilitating armed militants, leading to the assassination of a former prime minister. But, by March 1998, political turmoil at the Centre afforded Karunanidhi a breather. The Jain Commission's final report went soft on the DMK chief. *Outlook* magazine wrote this of the final report: 'Curiously, even as he lambasts the work of the CBI's Special Investigation Team – devoting an entire volume to its investigational lapses – Jain appears to have considerably toned down his earlier stand on the complicity of the DMK and has instead concentrated on the "foreign" angle.'[12]

While almost absolving Karunanidhi's government, Justice Jain took the plot behind Rajiv Gandhi's assassination abroad instead, pointing at the likelihood of the involvement of the CIA and the Mossad in ordering a hit on Gandhi. Jain also stated that a few individuals were likely to have been in the know about the assassination bid – godman Chandraswami, Subramanian Swamy, who was then with the Janata Party, and former Prime Minister Chandra Shekhar.

Karunanidhi was officially off the hook. He went on to save the NDA government under Prime Minister Atal Bihari Vajpayee in 1999.

2001: MIDNIGHT ARREST

In the wee hours of the morning of 30 June 2001, barely a month after AIADMK supremo Jayalalithaa had assumed charge as chief minister, she would wreak vengeance on her bête noire. At 1.45 a.m., a posse of policemen rudely woke up Karunanidhi at his Gopalapuram residence and shoved and dragged him down the stairs into a waiting jeep.

Remarkably, the Maran-owned Sun TV camera crew was in place during the midnight arrest, filming the entire spectacle. Karunanidhi, then seventy-seven, with his yellow shawl askew, was screaming, 'Kolraanga pa' – 'They are trying to kill me'. The video, which was aired repeatedly on Sun TV, created a wave of sympathy for the elderly man being hustled like a regular ruffian.

The unceremonious arrest was over allegations of corruption – the Flyover Scam, as it was popularly known – and purported embezzlement of Rs 12 crore by Karunanidhi and his son M.K. Stalin, who was then the mayor of Chennai. In the scuffle at Gopalapuram, Karunanidhi's nephew, Murasoli Maran, then Union minister for commerce and industry in the NDA cabinet, as well as T.R. Baalu, Union minister for environment and forests, were both injured and subsequently arrested by the Tamil Nadu police.

It was payback time for Jayalalithaa, who had been arrested in 1996 just after Karunanidhi assumed power, over allegations of corruption in the purchase of colour televisions for the government. The blowback, though, was strong. Jayalalithaa had not counted on the NDA government at the Centre, saved by the DMK, stepping in with pressure to undo her actions. Clear messages were sent out to the AIADMK that the arrest of Union ministers amounted to a constitutional crisis.

The *Hindu* reported on how Jayalalithaa was forced to back off, albeit reluctantly, within a week. 'First, the State decided to grant the two Union Ministers bail. When they refused to go out on bail, Ms Jayalalithaa dropped all charges against them in the interest of a "cordial relationship" with the Centre. And, though in the normal course Mr Karunanidhi might have had to spend as many days as she herself spent in jail, Ms Jayalalithaa ordered his release on bail on "purely humanitarian grounds" and taking into consideration the "advanced age" of the DMK leader.'[13] The case faded into oblivion thereafter.

THE 2G SCANDAL

The next test was perhaps the toughest of them all for Karunanidhi. An octogenarian by the time the 2G scandal hit the headlines, Karunanidhi would see his beloved daughter Kanimozhi go to jail and his ailing wife Dayalu Ammal face impending arrest. The chickens had come home to roost.

By May 2007, feuds had erupted within the DMK family, and the knives were out between Karunanidhi's elder son M.K. Alagiri and his grand-nephews, Kalanidhi and Dayanidhi Maran. As a result, Dayanidhi Maran, who was until then Karunanidhi's eyes and ears in Delhi, was forced to resign from his post as Union telecom minister in the UPA-I government and give way to a new favourite of Karunanidhi's – A. Raja. Kanimozhi supplanted the younger Maran as her father's representative in Delhi.

India had to move ahead to 2G or Second Generation telephony. For this, spectrum or airwaves vacated by the defence establishment would be used for the common populace. This is a regular feature – once defence moves on to the next generation communication spectrum, the redundant airwaves are handed over for the country's use.

It fell upon A. Raja to begin the process of allocation of this vacated 2G spectrum to various telecom companies. 2G was to bring in a communication revolution of sorts – it was meant to make phone calls cheaper, make mobile telephony more widely accessible to Indians and connect the country like never before.

In August 2007, the process of allotment of 2G spectrum to various interested telecom companies began. Bids were called for. The Telecom Regulatory Authority of India (TRAI) and the Department of Telecom (DoT), along with the minister, decided to follow the first-come-first-served method, instead of auctioning spectrum.

The interest was huge and over 575 applications had arrived from forty-six old and new players. On 25 September 2007, the telecom ministry fixed the deadline for applications as 1 October 2007. The prime minister and the finance ministry raised concerns over the procedure adopted by Raja – as per documents leaked to the media at the time.

On 10 January 2008, the DoT suddenly decided to advance the cut-off date for applications to 25 September from 1 October in retrospect.

By now the rumblings had begun and the media had smelt blood. Janata Party's Subramanian Swamy, who merged the party with the BJP in 2013, wrote to Prime Minister Manmohan Singh multiple times by November 2008. He sought permission to prosecute Raja over allegations of corruption in the issue of 2G licences.

The media across regions began taking the charges seriously. Raja and the telecom ministry, TRAI and other departments issued statements periodically, at pains to insist that they had gone by the rule book and that nothing was amiss.

This, though, would be the scandal, along with the coal block allocation scandal, that would drive the final nail in the UPA coffin in the 2014 elections.

When Manmohan Singh did not respond, Swamy took the 2G case to the Supreme Court, requesting sanction to prosecute

Raja. In 2009, the Central Vigilance Commission began a probe into the allegations of corruption in the case. By October 2009, the CBI had stepped in, under directions from the Supreme Court, filing an FIR against unknown officials of the DoT and unknown private companies. By September 2009, the Supreme Court had put a number to the alleged scam – Rs 70,000 crore.

A month later, the alleged scam exploded. The Comptroller Auditor General (CAG) report on 2G spectrum allocation was leaked to the media before it was tabled in Parliament. CAG Vinod Rai had pinned a mind-boggling figure to 2G – one lakh seventy-six thousand crore! The *New Indian Express*'s headline on 11 November 2010 was:

> Loss to the Nation
>
> 1760000000000
>
> Raja deprived govt of this much money in 2G spectrum allocation: CAG report

It was a figure simply too large to be comprehended, let alone ignored. The media pounced on the scandal with glee, conducting trials in television studios and inevitably finding Raja guilty over and over again. He was chased by cameras everywhere he went, hounded and accused by reporters in Delhi and Chennai. The media erupted in unison, pouring outrage over the 'biggest ever scam in Indian history'. The international media too picked up the scandal, shaming India over corruption.

The Opposition BJP and other parties blocked Parliament proceedings for weeks, clamouring for a probe into the alleged scam. The UPA-II government, weak-kneed and pushed to the wall, gave in, asking a protesting Raja to resign. Karunanidhi had no choice but to acquiesce, although he defended Raja strongly.

'Even before I could get into the issuance of licences or allocation of spectrum, one telecom bigwig, Sivasankaran [C. Sivasankaran, promoter of Aircel], approached the *Hindu* editor [N. Ram],' says Raja. 'Sivasankaran got jittery because we were following the "first come first served" model of spectrum allocation. He already had licences in some circles and had applied for the rest of the circles. He wanted an auction to be held so he could buy it. If not, he wanted a pan-India licence.

'Sivasankaran approached me also and I told him I want to be transparent,' says Raja. 'Once the cut-off date was advanced, my leader called me and said *Hindu* Ram spoke to me and said there was something wrong with the spectrum process. I then explained to Kalaignar all about spectrum and why we were not going in for an auction. Kalaignar understood immediately. He said that there will be pressure on you from bureaucrats. Even before we took a final decision on spectrum allocation, I had told Kalaignar about the whole process, our thinking and the plan.'

Karunanidhi, according to Raja, then told him to meet N. Ram. 'You may be a minister but he is a big man and you must show respect. Go to him and explain everything just the way you explained it to me' – was Karunanidhi's advice to Raja.

'I went straight to Ram's house and explained all over again,' says Raja. 'I even drew diagrams to simplify the concept. He accepted that there was nothing murky in this.'

"Afterwards, I again told my leader that this is a very dangerous step I was taking and that there would be trouble from a powerful telecom cartel that I was trying to break and that there would be a lot of heat,' continues Raja. 'Thalaivar simply said – go ahead and do what you have to. And he backed me all the way.'

When queried about this anecdote, N. Ram differs on the sequence of events. 'I did not have any request from Sivasankaran, absolutely not,' he says. 'What I heard from industry sources, including Sivasankaran, was that there was a big fix in the 2G spectrum policy. We knew the policy was going to be changed but we did not know the shape of it at that time. We did not know the date was going to be changed, to sort of fix the match, we had no details at that time. Industry sources told me there was going to be some sort of corrupt deal, some skullduggery if you like. I went to tell the Chief Minister Kalaignar about this. I don't want to reveal too much but he said he will explain to me. He called up Raja over the phone and told him – 'En peyara kedutthuraadha' (don't ruin my reputation).' Ram agrees that Raja spent several hours with him, explaining the entire 2G process.

But sacrifices must be made in politics and, perhaps, Raja was a smaller one. But more was to come. Linked to the 2G scandal was a Rs 200 crore loan given to Kalaignar TV, the DMK mouthpiece, through circuitous routes from some beneficiaries of 2G spectrum allocated by Raja. The director of the channel, at the time, was said to be Kanimozhi, Karunanidhi's daughter and Rajya Sabha MP.

As the CBI probed the deal, it described the loan as kickbacks for getting spectrum. Both Raja and Kanimozhi were jailed, the former for over a year and the latter for 190 days. Enforcement Directorate sleuths landed up in Karunanidhi's Gopalapuram home in the interim to question Dayalu Ammal, who was named as one of the directors in Kalaignar TV. This despite Karunanidhi asking for reprieve for his aged wife, who was reportedly suffering from Alzheimer's.

After seven long years of hearings, the CBI Court in Patiala House in Delhi pronounced the verdict on 21 December 2017. Judge O.P. Saini acquitted every one of the accused, stating in court, 'I have no hesitation in holding that the prosecution has failed to prove the charges beyond reasonable doubt. So all are acquitted.'

A. Raja subsequently released his book *The 2G Saga Unfolds* in January 2018, attacking former CAG Vinod Rai for political motives; Sunil Mittal, chairman, Bharti Enterprises; and then Solicitor General Goolam Vahanvati for placing him at the centre of what he calls a 'non-est scam'. He wrote with respect of then Prime Minister Manmohan Singh, who, he said, supported him all along the way but that some other members of UPA-II let him down.

Karunanidhi, who was by then confined to his wheelchair, a tracheostomy tube down his throat, unable to speak but whose mind continued to work as sharply as ever, smiled at Raja. Father and daughter celebrated with a selfie.

7

TAKING CENTRE STAGE

A trip to Delhi was imminent. As Karunanidhi took over as chief minister for the first time in March 1969, he travelled along with Law Minister S. Madhavan by air from Madras. In the national capital, they, along with DMK MPs, headed to meet Prime Minister Indira Gandhi as well as her cabinet.

A warm welcome awaited the young team. Following what was, in his own words, a pleasant forty-minute meeting with Mrs Gandhi, Karunanidhi then met and charmed other ministers, including External Affairs Minister Dinesh Singh and Home Minister Yashwantrao Chavan. Karunanidhi recounts how Food Minister Babu Jagjivan Ram embraced him with warmth and, as per Karunanidhi's demand, immediately sanctioned 10,000 tonnes of rice as a first instalment. He also gave approval for setting up three sugar mills in the state.[1]

Karunanidhi then sensed that large cracks were beginning to open within the grand old party. The warmth of the Indira team was not shown by Deputy Prime Minister and Finance Minister Morarji Desai. As the Karunanidhi entourage arrived five minutes late to his residence, thanks to an unforeseen traffic snarl, Desai was visibly fuming.

'How long do I wait for you? Do you think I have no other work?' snapped Desai at the group. Karunanidhi writes about how they were taken aback. When Desai asked them to have a seat, Karunanidhi writes that he sat down in a chair as if it were filled with thorns. As decided, the young chief minister asked the Union finance minister to sanction Rs 5 crore for the state. Karunanidhi recounts what happened next.

Desai's face reddened.

'I do not have a tree in my orchard that grows money,' said Desai.

'Trees that grow money do not exist – how can they be in your orchard?' retorted Karuna.

Within minutes of that exchange, the Tamil Nadu group left. Desai subsequently attempted to make peace that same night at a dinner organized for the Tamil Nadu leaders.

But Karunanidhi had sniffed trouble brewing. It came in the form of communist leader Bhupesh Gupta and a young Congress leader, Chandra Shekhar, questioning the deputy prime minister in Parliament about his budget sops that allegedly favoured the Birla group. Chandra Shekhar also showed how Desai's daughter-in-law and her two minor children were shareholders of a company linked to the Birlas. A furious Desai attempted to shout the opposition from within his party down. Chandra Shekhar shouted back, stating that in the House, all were equal and had the right to question anyone. Desai demanded of Indira Gandhi that she take action against Chandra Shekhar.[2]

This was the beginning of the rift. As the old guard of the Congress – Morarji Desai, K. Kamaraj and others – closed ranks,

Indira and her team forged ahead. Karunanidhi cleverly chose to back the lady.

The first test of Karunanidhi and the DMK's loyalty to the Indira Gandhi faction would be during the 1969 presidential elections. When President Zakir Husain died on 3 May 1969, Vice President V.V. Giri took charge as Acting President. 'The senior leaders of the Congress were working hard to ensure that the next president would not be someone who would work well with Indira Gandhi,' writes Karunanidhi.[3]

Then Punjab chief minister, Gurnam Singh, met with Karunanidhi to discuss whom he would support for the presidential candidacy. As names flew back and forth from various quarters, the All India Congress Committee met to decide upon a candidate. The options were Giri, Neelam Sanjiva Reddy and Babu Jagjivan Ram. Reddy was the choice of then Congress president S. Nijalingappa as well as Morarji Desai and the senior leaders. Indira Gandhi and Fakhruddin Ali Ahmed were the only two members who initially supported Giri and later Jagjivan Ram. They were vetoed and the Congress announced Reddy as its presidential candidate. The swords were crossed.

Karunanidhi, while touring Thanjavur district, recounts how reporters quizzed him for his comments on the selection of Reddy as the Congress party's presidential candidate. Karunanidhi used the opportunity to make his stand clear: 'I feel this decision is a big let-down, and during Mahatma Gandhi's birth centenary, they should have made a Dalit the president, a wish that Gandhi always had. They should have made Babu Jagjivan Ram the president,' he said.

Indira Gandhi and her allies got the hint. Bhupesh Gupta, the CPI leader, in July 1969, met Karunanidhi and held talks. They resolved that the DMK, the CPI and the CPM would back Giri for the president's post.

Karunanidhi then wrote a letter to leaders of all Opposition parties, extending an invitation to them for a meeting in Madras, Delhi or any place of their choice to discuss the issue of the next president. The invitation was accepted and Delhi was chosen as the venue for the meeting.

On 16 July, Indira Gandhi suddenly removed Desai from his post as finance minister, stating that he would, however, continue as deputy prime minister. On 19 July, an ordinance was passed by the Union cabinet to nationalize banks in the country. Acting President V.V. Giri signed the ordinance.

On 21 July, Karunanidhi arrived in Delhi to lobby with the Opposition leaders over the presidential candidate. Over the next two days, Karunanidhi held talks with the CPI's Bhupesh Gupta, Atal Bihari Vajpayee, Praja Socialist Party's S.N. Dwivedy and Madhu Limaye, George Fernandes, West Bengal Chief Minister Ajoy Mukherjee and Deputy CM Jyoti Basu, Punjab Chief Minister Gurnam Singh, the Indian Muslim League's leader Qaid-e Millath, V.K. Krishna Menon and others.

Everyone was convinced that Indira Gandhi would support Giri against Reddy as president. But, on the evening of 22 July 1969, Indira Gandhi and Defence Minister Swaran Singh submitted the nominations for Reddy. On 26 July, back in Madras, Karunanidhi announced that the DMK, along with the CPI, CPM, Socialist Party, Muslim League and the Akali Dal would support the candidacy of Giri.

On 30 July, the Congress committee demanded that the prime minister write to all Congress MPs asking them to vote for Reddy. She declined to do so. 'If V.V. Giri had lost the election, the senior leaders in the Congress would have become more powerful and she would have had to resign as prime minister – this was the talk within political circles at the time. This was the reason

Indira Gandhi was forced to go against the leadership in such a surreptitious manner,' writes Karunanidhi.[4]

The presidential election was held on 16 August 1969. Votes were counted on 20 August 1969. Giri won the election by a margin of 14,500 votes. From Tamil Nadu's MPs and MLAs, Giri got 35,448 votes. 'If you compare the votes, it is clear that if V.V. Giri had not got Tamil Nadu's votes, Sanjiva Reddy would have become president,' crows Karunanidhi.[5] He goes on to say that if he and the DMK had taken a different decision, Indira Gandhi would have, figuratively, bitten the dust.

FEDERALISM AND STATE AUTONOMY

On 12 February 1975, the Lion of Kashmir, Sheikh Abdullah, visited Karunanidhi at his home in Madras for breakfast. The two spoke in earnest about the need to ensure state autonomy from the Centre and entrench the federal character of the Constitution.

In 1969, the DMK government had constituted a committee headed by retired high court judge P.V. Rajamannar. Other members of this committee were the then vice chancellor of Madras University, A. Lakshmanaswami Mudaliar, and retired judge Chandra Reddy. This committee went into great detail about how to make states more autonomous, clearly delineating Centre–state powers and suggesting resolutions to conflicting or confusing issues surrounding federalism. After much discussion over the report submitted by the committee, on 20 April 1974, the state assembly passed a resolution accepting the suggestions in the Rajamannar Committee report and demanded autonomy for states. Tamil Nadu was the first state in the country to pass such a resolution.

It would take eight years for other states to catch up. In 1983, Karnataka Chief Minister Ramakrishna Hegde of the Janata Party picked up the Rajamannar Committee report and organized a meeting of the chief ministers of the southern states to speak on state autonomy. In the same year, Farooq Abdullah, the son of Sheikh Abdullah, who was by then chief minister of Jammu and Kashmir, held a public meeting with chief ministers of many states including, N.T. Rama Rao of Andhra Pradesh (Telugu Desam Party) and Jyoti Basu of West Bengal (CPM). In this meeting too, the DMK government's resolution on state autonomy would be hailed and reiterated.

ARM-TWISTING THE CENTRE

The judiciary and the prime minister clashed on two important decisions taken by the Centre that were successively struck down by the apex court in 1969-70. Indira Gandhi's move to nationalize banks and abolish the privy purse were both challenged and struck down – the court held that the legislature had the right to nationalize banks but payments being made after ten years in the form of bonds was not acceptable. This precipitated mid-term general elections in 1971.

Indira Gandhi, who had split the Congress and was at loggerheads with the judiciary, was on a sticky wicket. She needed allies to come back to power. In December 1969, she invited Karunanidhi to meet with her in Delhi to discuss elections and an alliance. The meeting, according to Karunanidhi, lasted an hour. Upon returning to Madras, the DMK executive committee met and decided to dissolve the assembly and go in for elections along with the Centre.

On 5 January 1970, Chief Minister Karunanidhi submitted a letter to the governor of the state, requesting that the assembly be dissolved and the state go to polls along with the Centre. When reporters queried Karunanidhi as to why he took this decision, he replied, 'The entire country is going to polls to elect members of the Parliament. It is true that our government can continue for another year in power. But if there are elections every year and leaders keep changing, it will affect governance and, ultimately, the people. We have taken this decision in public interest,' he said.[6]

The alliance for the state was firmed up – Indira's Congress, the DMK, both Left parties, Praja Socialist Party, Tamilarasu Kazhagam, Muslim League and the Forward Bloc. On 8 January 1970, they met to decide upon seat allocation. On 19 January, Indira Gandhi arrived in Madras and an hour-long discussion ensued.

'We were willing to allocate Indira Congress five to seven parliamentary seats and ten to fifteen assembly seats,' said Karunanidhi to the waiting press after the meeting ended. 'This is more than what we have given the other parties in the alliance. But the Indira Congress leaders are not satisfied. Thus, talks have broken down,' he announced. He added that the DMK, which had contested 170 seats in the 1967 assembly polls, wished to contest more seats in 1971.

The Congress needed the DMK, and Karunanidhi knew it better than anyone else. Senior Congressman and former chief minister of Madras State M. Bhaktavatsalam arrived to meet Karunanidhi along with C. Subramaniam and Mohan Kumaramangalam. The demand was for over eighty assembly seats and more than twenty Lok Sabha seats for Indira's Congress in Tamil Nadu. Karunanidhi flatly refused, sticking to his original offer. An infuriated Bhaktavatsalam announced that the talks were over. Karunanidhi recounts C. Subramaniam as saying: 'This is a challenge to our self-respect.' At this, Karunanidhi laughed: 'Our movement is all about Self Respect.'[7]

Tamil Nadu's Indira Congress wing went ahead and released a list of candidates for the state. Karunanidhi followed suit, announcing the DMK's candidate list at a rally on 24 July 1970.

Karunanidhi recounts how he almost brought the redoubtable Indira Gandhi to her knees.

> Around midnight, the phone rang. It was Prime Minister Indira Gandhi and G. Parthasarathy from Delhi.
>
> 'Why has such a thing happened?' they asked regretfully.
>
> 'We have not made any mistake. Your Tamil Nadu Congress unit released their list of candidates. It is only after that that we released our list.' I replied.
>
> 'Would you reconsider your decision and give us at least twenty assembly seats and ten Lok Sabha seats?' they asked.
>
> 'It is not possible to allocate assembly seats any longer but I will think about whether I can give some parliamentary seats,' I said.[8]

Karunanidhi got more than what he had bargained for. The Congress (I) was effectively kept out of the state and he threw a few crumbs their way – ten Lok Sabha seats in Tamil Nadu. Mrs Gandhi had no choice but to accept it.

She would, though, have her revenge a few years later.

In March 1971, the country went to polls. Indira Gandhi returned as prime minister and Karunanidhi as chief minister of Tamil Nadu. The victory was historic – it was the first time ever that a party had won over 180 assembly seats in the 234-member House.

INDIRA AND MGR VERSUS KARUNANIDHI

Karunanidhi recalls how MGR, who was then shooting for a film in Kashmir, rushed to Delhi and called him from there to wish him on the monumental success. Karunanidhi says that MGR asked him for a berth in the cabinet – the 'medical ministry' – referring to the health portfolio. 'You come immediately. We will speak in person,' said Karunanidhi to him. There were no flights available, so MGR chartered a private flight and landed in Madras.[9]

Karunanidhi goes on to describe how he, Law Minister Madhavan, and Nedunchezhiyan tried to tell MGR that he could not become a minister unless he gave up his acting career. Karunanidhi alleges that MGR was stubborn in his refusal to give up his cine stardom, as mentioned in an earlier chapter. Karunanidhi says that MGR did not show his anger overtly but buried it deep within his heart and gave up his demand for a ministerial berth.

An angered Indira and an infuriated MGR boded ill for Karunanidhi, riding high on a string of successes. Karunanidhi writes, 'Hidden away and stoked by Delhi, the treachery would take full form in September 1972.'[10]

In August 1972, another incident, narrated by Karunanidhi, widened the rift between him and MGR. A public meeting was scheduled to be held on 5 and 6 August in Madurai. Karunanidhi writes about MGR visiting him at his residence to make a specific request – that an actor who had been a heroine in many of his films be given membership in the DMK, that she be seated in the front row on stage at the public meeting at Madurai and she be mentioned in the welcome address. 'Eh Appa! The Dravida movement cannot withstand this – think patiently,' Karunanidhi is said to have told MGR.[11] MGR was referring to the young cine star Jayalalithaa.

At the Madurai public meeting, MGR condemned the Centre and heaped praise on the DMK government, hailing its 'clean governance'. MGR ended his speech with a war cry:

MGR: State autonomy…
People: We will beget at any cost…
MGR: Tamil Nadu government…

People: We will protect! We will protect!

MGR: Under the leadership of Kalaignar…

People: We will follow…[12]

Though MGR spoke vehemently in support of Karunanidhi and the DMK government, in September 1972 he did a U-turn, as detailed in an earlier chapter. At a public rally in Madras, MGR attacked Karunanidhi, accusing the DMK and its ministers of corruption and demanded that they show accounts of their wealth to the people. The DMK expelled MGR. With that was born the ADMK, with about half the cadre leaving the party to follow their matinee idol.

As the DMK was struggling with its intra-party rebellion, 1975 arrived and, with it, the Emergency. The DMK, which was in alliance with Indira's Congress, was one of the most strident voices condemning the imposition of Emergency in the country. On 12 June 1975, the Allahabad High Court ruled that Indira Gandhi's disputed election from Rae Bareilly in Uttar Pradesh in the 1971 election was null and void. The court agreed that Gandhi had resorted to corrupt practices in order to win the seat. A clamour began for Gandhi's resignation as prime minister. 'If she had resigned on her own, we would have lauded it,' Karunanidhi told reporters.[13]

On 25 June, days before a countrywide protest was to be held by Opposition parties led by Morarji Desai, President Fakhruddin Ali Ahmed, at the behest of Prime Minister Indira Gandhi, declared Emergency under Article 352 of the Indian Constitution. With Karunanidhi's open and relentless condemnation of the Emergency and its excesses, relations between Gandhi and the Tamil Nadu chief minister worsened. An enemy's enemy must be a friend. In this case, MGR and Indira Gandhi came closer in order to beat a common enemy. Hundreds of DMK party workers were arrested and Tamil Nadu was seen as a safe haven for those being targeted by an oppressive regime at the Centre. Under the DMK's benevolent watch, magazines, pamphlets and other material condemning the Emergency were printed and circulated to other states. Karunanidhi's son M.K. Stalin was arrested and beaten while in jail.

The DMK government was subsequently dismissed in 1976 by Indira Gandhi, citing corruption allegations on the basis of MGR's letters to the President of India. The 1977 elections saw a new alliance emerge between Indira's Congress and MGR's ADMK. The DMK allied with the Janata Party headed by Morarji Desai.

DESAI AND CHANDRA SHEKHAR DAYS

Desai became prime minister in 1977. The MGR charisma, though, outshone Karunanidhi's persona and he lost the chief minister's chair to his old friend who had since turned foe. Karunanidhi remained in Opposition until MGR died in December 1987.

Within a year, however, the motley group that was the Janata Party began quibbling amongst themselves. At a parliamentary committee meeting in Delhi, Home Affairs Minister Charan Singh and External Affairs Minister A.B. Vajpayee demanded that action be taken against some members of the party who had spoken out against them. Janata Party president Chandra Shekhar and Prime Minister Morarji Desai attempted to soothe the ruffled feathers. But the party went out of control. Charan Singh, Defence Minister Babu Jagjivan Ram and Prime Minister Desai were at loggerheads.

At a public meeting held by the Janata Party in Chandigarh, Desai warned that he would resign as prime minister within six months unless the intra-party feuds subsided. In 1978, Charan Singh resigned and later withdrew his resignation.

In July 1979, Opposition parties brought a no-confidence motion against Desai. The Indira Congress would obviously oppose the government. But, surprisingly, the ADMK, an ally, announced that they would support the Centre at the vote.

Charan Singh's machinations worked and close to sixty-four MPs of the erstwhile Lok Dal resigned from the Janata Party and joined Raj Narain's Janata Party (S), bringing the numbers of the ruling Janata Party down to 238 from the original 302 MPs they had in 1977. Raj Narain then announced that they were willing to form the government with the backing of the Indira Congress, if they so desired. The Left announced their desire to vote against the Desai government.

Faced with a jam, Deputy Prime Minister Jagjivan Ram, on 15 July 1979, met with the prime minister and spoke to him for an hour. He explained to Desai that the majority of members within the Janata Party did not wish for him to hold the post. Desai agreed to step down as prime minister. That same day at 6.30 p.m., he submitted his resignation to the president.

On 28 July 1979, Charan Singh was sworn in as prime minister, backed by the Indira Congress. Within three weeks of taking charge, he inducted ADMK MPs Sathyavani Muthu and Bala Pazhanoor as ministers in his cabinet. One day after that, he requested the president to dissolve the government and hold fresh mid-term polls. Singh had realized that Indira Gandhi would not support his government at the pending vote of confidence.

BACK WITH INDIRA

Karunanidhi acted swiftly, knowing that the balance of power had, once again, tipped towards the side of the Indira Congress. In September 1979, after a botched attempt at merging the DMK and the ADMK, Karunanidhi, along with Thennarasu and Arcot Veerasamy, headed to Delhi to meet with Indira Gandhi. An alliance was firmed up, with DMK agreeing to contest seventeen seats in Tamil Nadu in the mid-term polls scheduled for November

1979, the Indira Congress contesting twenty-two. Indira Gandhi gave speeches and interviews to the press denouncing MGR and his ADMK as being 'opportunists'.[14]

Karnataka Chief Minister Devaraj Urs slammed the alliance, stating that the DMK had turned to Indira Gandhi in order to escape from the Sarkaria Commission charges. Karunanidhi retorted that if Urs could form an alliance with Charan Singh, who had initiated the Grover Commission against him, then there was nothing wrong with the DMK allying with the Indira Congress. In January 1980, Indira Gandhi romped home to power with 351 out of 525 seats.

In February 1980, buoyed by the huge win of the alliance at the Centre, the DMK and the Indira Congress members took out a rally from Kamaraj statue on Anna Salai to Raj Bhavan in Madras. They handed over a list of irregularities and accusations against the ADMK government to the governor.

Around 9 p.m. on the night of 17 February 1980, the Union cabinet held an urgent meeting to discuss the dismissal of nine state governments which were not ruled by the Congress or its allies. This included the ADMK government in Tamil Nadu. President Sanjiva Reddy signed the order and the ADMK government was dismissed and President's Rule imposed on the state. Karunanidhi had his revenge on MGR.

By April 1980, it was time for seat sharing talks again, this time for the state assembly polls. As talks were being held between the DMK and Indira Congress in Chennai, a mysterious story was put out by the Press Trust of India – that if the DMK-Indira Congress combine won, the chief minister's post would go to the DMK and that both parties had agreed on contesting an equal number of assembly seats. Karunanidhi was flummoxed.

At the same time, some Congressmen from Tamil Nadu were in Delhi, attempting to convince Gandhi that in the event of a victory, the chief minister should be from the Congress party. Congress's Tamil Nadu in-charge Ram Gopal Reddy told reporters that a decision on who would be chief minister would be made only after the polls. The DMK stopped talks with the Indira Congress midway, until Gandhi herself announced that there was no confusion as regards the fact that the DMK would get the chief minister's chair in the event of victory.

On 25 April 1980, the list of candidates was released. The DMK and the Indira Congress would contest 113 seats each and the Muslim League would contest eight. Out of the Congress's 113 seats, four went to smaller allies. In-fighting broke out in the Congress, with those denied seats refusing to campaign for the alliance. The DMK's younger members too were deeply disappointed as, in the final count, with a few more allies, the party ended up contesting a mere 109 seats.

In May 1980, matinee idol MGR once again bested Karunanidhi and became chief minister.

THE ASSASSINATION OF INDIRA GANDHI

On 31 October 1984, violence hit the streets of north India as Indira Gandhi's Sikh bodyguards assassinated her over Operation Blue Star, which she had spearheaded and which had devastated the holy Golden Temple in Amritsar while flushing out the armed separatists holed up inside. Anti-Sikh riots followed in Punjab and in the national capital. Karunanidhi condemned the violence.

On 5 October 1984, MGR had taken ill and a month later was flown to New York for hospitalization there. With the passing of Indira Gandhi, general elections were scheduled for December 1984.

With MGR unwell and a sympathy wave for the assassinated Indira Gandhi, the young, ambitious politician J. Jayalalithaa flew to Delhi to meet Rajiv Gandhi. An alliance was on the table, along with an offer to conduct both the general and Tamil Nadu elections together. The DMK was left holding hands with the Left parties and the Indian Union Muslim League.

The arithmetic worked in the ADMK's favour and the Congress party was back in power at the Centre and MGR sworn in as chief minister for the third time in 1984. The victory was short-lived. MGR breathed his last on 24 December 1987.

A BRIEF INTERLUDE

Following MGR's death, the state descended into chaos. A succession war broke out between MGR's wife Janaki Ramachandran and the charismatic cine star and propaganda secretary of the party, J. Jayalalithaa. Nedunchezhiyan, who was acting chief minister, paved the way for Janaki, who was sworn in as chief minister. But her government lasted a mere twenty-three days, from 7 to 30 January 1988.

Citing a complete breakdown of law and order, in the wake of violent assembly sessions, President's Rule was once again clamped down upon the state.

In 1989 came elections yet again – assembly elections in Tamil Nadu in January and parliamentary polls in November. By then, Karunanidhi and the DMK had joined the National Front alliance with N.T. Rama Rao, V.P. Singh, Chandra Shekhar, Biju Patnaik, I.K. Gujral, Surjit Singh Barnala and others. The first public rally of the National Front took place in Madras on 17 September 1988. The ADMK continued in its alliance with the Indira Congress.

Karunanidhi's time had come after ten long years. The DMK rode back to power in Tamil Nadu along with the National Front at the Centre. Karunanidhi became chief minister once more. And V.P. Singh took over as prime minister later that year.

On 12 June 1990, Singh wrote to all chief ministers asking for their suggestions on implementing the recommendations of the Mandal Commission. The DMK was a staunch supporter of the caste-based reservations recommended by it. Karunanidhi had, even before the Commission was set up to look into the issue of reservation and reforms, made a fervent pitch for the same in 1973. Karunanidhi recounts his speech at a meeting of backward and oppressed classes held in Allahabad on 14 October 1973: 'The Centre has reserved employment opportunities in government only for the oppressed classes. This reservation should be extended to the backward classes as well. I request the Centre to implement this,' he had said.[15]

As the Mandal Commission recommendations – caste-based and population-based reservations – were ratified by Parliament, protests broke out in north India as the forward castes took to the streets in anger. The DMK and Karunanidhi were the rock on which the Mandal reforms were pushed through and defended in their entirety.

V.P. Singh, though, did not last long. The coalition government, which had outside support from the Bharatiya Janata Party (BJP), could not afford to antagonize its allies who afforded it a fragile majority.

In July 1990, Deputy Prime Minister Devi Lal gave an interview to the magazine *Illustrated Weekly of India*, charging a number of Union ministers with corruption. Prime Minister V.P. Singh demanded that his deputy present him with evidence. Devi Lal kept his silence. As a result, Singh removed him from the post of deputy prime minister on 1 August 1990.

Karunanidhi recounts an urgent telephone call from his counterpart N.T. Rama Rao of Andhra Pradesh the same day. Rao wanted Karunanidhi to take the first flight to Hyderabad the next morning and join him en route to Delhi to hold talks as the crisis appeared to be intensifying. Karunanidhi complied.

Both leaders arrived in Delhi and were informed that the prime minister wished to speak with them. Talks went on until midnight of 2 August. It was decided that no one would replace Devi Lal as deputy prime minister. The National Front met and reposed faith in Singh's prime ministership.

But the problems continued in the form of L.K. Advani, a leader of the BJP, who had embarked on a rath yatra to garner support to build a Ram temple at the disputed Babri Masjid site in Ayodhya. Despite the National Front's dissent and Prime Minister V.P. Singh's warnings not to go ahead with the yatra as it was causing communal violence across the country, the BJP, on 17 October 1990, resolved that if the rath yatra or the building of the Ram temple in Ayodhya was stopped, they would withdraw outside support to the National Front government.

On 22 October 1990, Advani was arrested at Samastipur in Bihar as his rath yatra arrived. The BJP withdrew support immediately and the National Front government lost its majority in Parliament. Chandra Shekhar, who had been a harsh critic of V.P. Singh, used the opportunity to ensure that voices of dissent against the prime minister only became louder.

In November 1990, the Janata Dal split into two, with Chandra Shekhar taking sixty-eight MPs with him and V.P. Singh being left with eighty-three. Chandra Shekhar then struck a deal with Rajiv Gandhi's Congress (I) and assumed charge as prime minister on 10 November 1990, with Devi Lal as deputy prime minister.

But Karunanidhi had voted in favour of V.P. Singh during the confidence motion in Parliament which Singh ultimately lost. Chandra Shekhar did not forget this. And his crucial ally, Rajiv Gandhi's Congress (I) in alliance with the ADMK, would not rest easy either.

MORE TURMOIL IN STATE AND CENTRE

Rumours abounded that the DMK government was to be dismissed soon. The press was agog with curiosity, asking the chief minister repeatedly what was going on and whether he had heard that his government was likely to be dismissed. Jayalalithaa made frequent trips to Delhi to meet Rajiv Gandhi and other leaders during this period.

Karunanidhi writes that he got a call from then External Affairs Minister V.C. Shukla, asking to meet with him in Madras on 28 January 1991. Shukla wanted Karunanidhi's opinion on dealing with the Sri Lankan issue before heading to Colombo for talks the next day. Shukla met Karunanidhi at Madurai and the two held a long discussion on the crisis. Karunanidhi recounts how reporters surrounded him after Shukla left, asserting that the state government could not possibly be on the verge of dismissal since the Centre was so cordial with the state.

The next day, Tamil Nadu Governor Surjit Singh Barnala was summoned to Delhi and, by Karunanidhi's account, asked to dismiss the DMK government. Barnala refused to comply. V.P. Singh and his faction of the National Front got wind of the plan and rushed to meet the president to stop the dismissal. Nothing worked. Since the governor refused, under Article 356, the president stepped in and imposed President's Rule, dismissing the DMK government and the entire assembly on 30 January 1991. The dismissal was over allegations that the DMK government was encouraging the LTTE and other militant groups and providing them with safe passage and shelter in the state.

The Centre would not last very long either. On 5 March 1991, the Congress (I) angrily walked out of Parliament, demanding to know who had ordered two policemen to spy on Rajiv Gandhi's home.

Just before the walkout, DMK MP Murasoli Maran spoke of the prime minister thus. 'Prime Minister Chandra Shekhar appears to be willing to pay any price for the Congress. Since there are Haryana policemen spying outside Rajiv Gandhi's house, if the Congress asks him to dismiss the Haryana government, he will do it. Do you know what the people of India are saying now? They say that if the Congress asks Chandra Shekhar to immediately remove his beard, he would do so. Respected Prime Minister, your long-time wish has been fulfilled. You have become prime minister. There will only be a footnote about you in history, not even a whole sentence. I ask Chandra Shekhar – Please Get Out! How long are you going to suffer this humiliation?' he said.[16] Maran was taking a dig at the Speaker, who had asked MPs to 'get out' of the House.

'In parliamentary language, I am asking you to step down from your post. Because they [the Congress] are asking you to do all sorts of things that go against your own conscience. Therefore, it is better if you step down and meet the people,' said Maran.

The next day, a furious Chandra Shekhar, after stating that he was not a 'puppet of the Congress (I) party which kept him in power', submitted his resignation to President R. Venkataraman.

Elections loomed yet again. Polls for the Lok Sabha were slated for May 1991, while those for the state assembly were scheduled for June. On 21 May 1991, as Rajiv Gandhi was touring Tamil Nadu, campaigning for his party and alliance with the ADMK under Jayalalithaa's leadership, the unthinkable happened. He was assassinated by a suicide squad of the LTTE.

The shock and its subsequent sympathy wave, coupled with the allegations that Karunanidhi had encouraged and nourished the LTTE, all worked in Jayalalithaa's favour. From 1991 to 1996, Jayalalithaa was in charge of the state as chief minister for the first time. The Congress party too came to power at the Centre in a coalition. P.V. Narasimha Rao became prime minister and completed his full five-year term in office. He also initiated the Jain Commission of Inquiry into Karunanidhi's and the DMK government's activities supporting terror on Tamil soil.

In 1992, as the hurricane of the Babri Masjid demolition was gathering pace, the DMK began conducting protests and public meetings condemning the intent of the kar sevaks. Chief Minister Jayalalithaa lent her support to the building of the Ram temple. On 5 December 1992, Karunanidhi wrote in his party organ *Murasoli*:

> What does Kar Seva mean?
> Service to God? Or
> The service of sowing the seeds of unrest?
> And a maiden here to lend a hand to this deed?
> (Lord) Raman was born in the Treta Yuga
> Dvapara Yuga arrived; and has been crossed,
> When one says this is Kali Yuga
> It means 20 lakh years have gone by!
> So many lakhs of years ago
> Wonder who has seen the birthplace of Raman? Who has written it?
> Now by insisting that *this* is the exact place
> Where is the justice in demolishing Islamic history?
> In Ayodhya town a temple for Raman
> Without reservation, to be built
> We all agree; but to do that
> If you say we will demolish Babri Masjid, we will not agree!

The next day, though, kar sevaks entered and demolished the Babri Masjid. 'For not taking steps to prevent such a dastardly deed, the Centre will have to take full responsibility for what is going to happen,' wrote Karunanidhi in a statement.[17] As he had predicted, the country went up in communal flames.

Shortly thereafter, in 1995, Chief Minister Jayalalithaa dug her own political grave in the form of the ostentatious wedding for her foster son, V.N. Sudhakaran, who was also her close friend and confidante Sasikala Natarajan's nephew. In 1996, the people of Tamil Nadu brought her down and Karunanidhi was back in business. There would be no further dismissals of state governments of Tamil Nadu, which would alternately complete their full terms under the DMK and the AIADMK.

Not so with the Centre. In 1996, Jayalalithaa, in Opposition in the state, continued with the Congress. By 1996, the DMK had decided to move out of V.P. Singh's National Front alliance, stating that they were upset about the Front's attempts to bring the Jayalalithaa-led AIADMK in. The DMK contested the 1996 parliamentary polls with the CPI and a breakaway faction of the Tamil Nadu Congress led by G.K. Moopanar, which was called the Tamil Maanila Congress.

REGIONAL PARTIES HOLD SWAY

A hung Parliament meant a dire need for support from regional parties like the DMK. After being sworn in as chief minister on 13 May 1996, the very next day, Karunanidhi flew to Delhi following insistent and urgent summons from the Telugu Desam Party chief and Andhra Pradesh Chief Minister Chandrababu Naidu and other leaders. A meeting was called at the Tamil Nadu House and attended by West Bengal Chief Minister Jyoti Basu, CPM General Secretary Harkishan Singh Surjeet, CPI General Secretary Indrajit Gupta, Bihar Chief Minister Lalu Prasad Yadav, former Uttar Pradesh Chief Minister Mulayam Singh Yadav, former Union minister Madhavrao Scindia, TMC leader Moopanar, Chandrababu Naidu, P. Chidambaram, Karnataka Chief Minister H.D. Deve Gowda and others.

Following this, the team visited the home of V.P. Singh, leader of the National Front, and offered their support to him if he were to become prime minister. Singh declined.[18] The group trooped back to Tamil Nadu House and discussions continued. H.D. Deve Gowda was finally decided upon as the prime ministerial candidate. This motley group of regional parties, the first non-Congress, non-BJP alliance, was called the United Front.

President Shankar Dayal Sharma invited the BJP's leader, Atal Bihari Vajpayee, to form the government and prove his majority in the House, since theirs was the coalition with the largest number of votes. On 27 May 1996, the BJP front faced a confidence vote in Parliament. While speaking at the debate in the House, the DMK's Murasoli Maran said:

> Respected Speaker, I am very sorrowful that I am forced to speak against the motion brought in today by Mr Atal Bihari Vajpayee. I do not have less affection for him. But I have more affection for my people, my language, my culture, brothers and sisters and my society. If the Honourable President had first made enquiries about the support for Mr Vajpayee before swearing him in as Prime Minister, the situation would have been different. Unfortunately, that has not happened. We have immense respect and regard for Mr Vajpayee. As our leader Kalaignar has said, he is a great man. But he is in the wrong party. He is a lofty parliamentarian. He has very special qualities, which make him apt to be a prime minister. But the ideology that has brought him forward is something that we need to be forewarned about. This is why we are opposing the confidence motion.[19]

Maran suggested that Vajpayee himself resign rather than face the vote. Before the voting could take place, Vajpayee did just that. He resigned after thirteen days as prime minister on 28 May 1996. That same night, Deve Gowda met President Sharma and staked claim to form the government. Narasimha Rao of the Congress informed the president that they would support the United Front government at the vote. On 1 June 1996, Deve Gowda was sworn in as the twelfth Prime Minister of India. With him was sworn in the DMK's Murasoli Maran as labour minister, T.G. Venkatraman as minister for surface transport (independent charge) and the TMC's P. Chidambaram as finance minister.

It was the bonhomie between Chandrababu Naidu and Karunanidhi during this period that would help him ink a pact with Andhra Pradesh for the Telugu Ganga project and allocation of Krishna water for the parched northern Tamil Nadu, specifically Chennai.

Any delicate coalition is prone to bickering and the Congress, which provided outside support to the United Front, in April 1997 pulled the rug from under the feet of Deve Gowda. As polls were imminent, a compromise was quickly drawn up – the United Front would put up an alternative prime minister, since Deve Gowda and the Congress had faced friction. I.K. Gujral was chosen to lead the nation as the compromise candidate of the United Front government, with the Congress agreeing to continue outside support.

Within eight months, though, this government too fell, with Bihar Chief Minister Lalu Prasad Yadav walking out of the United Front alliance. The Congress's demand of dropping the DMK from the alliance on the basis of the Jain Commission's interim report, which dealt with Rajiv Gandhi's assassination, was refused by the Gujral government. The interim report had stated that the DMK had links with the LTTE. The Congress once again withdrew support.

SUCCESSIVE HUNG PARLIAMENTS

Polls beckoned yet again and the Parliament was hung. The BJP, with the AIADMK's Jayalalithaa in tow, managed to come back to power, again in a coalition, and Vajpayee was made prime minister. The DMK remained with the United Front. The Vajpayee-led government lasted thirteen months. When Jayalalithaa's demand that the DMK government in Tamil Nadu be sacked was not heeded by Vajpayee, she pulled the plug in 1999 and withdrew support of her eighteen MPs in Parliament. Vajpayee lost the confidence motion in Parliament by a single vote, thanks to the 'No' vote of Orissa Chief Minister Giridhar Gamang – whose right to vote in Parliament Vajpayee himself had batted for.

In September-October 1999, the country went to polls yet again. The National Democratic Alliance (NDA) was formed, with the DMK in alliance. On 13 October 1999, Vajpayee was sworn in as prime minister and the government finally completed the five-year term. The DMK landed three ministerial berths, with Murasoli Maran, T.R. Baalu and A. Raja joining the Vajpayee cabinet.

But the DMK and Karunanidhi later regretted the alliance. 'He has told us many times that he should not have gone with the BJP, especially after the Godhra killings and riots,' says Raja. 'He told me once that they have converted Hindutva, which is a school of thought, into a religious anthem. But he had given his word that he would remain in the alliance for five years. It was a political promise and he said he had to keep it.'

The DMK lost its vote share in the future assembly polls, as the AIADMK under Jayalalithaa gained in strength. The future of Tamil Nadu's governments too rested on alliances with caste-based parties that garnered and held on to small but significant vote shares.

THE CONGRESS ONCE AGAIN

In 2001, Jayalalithaa came back to power. In 2006, Karunanidhi became chief minister. It was in this term that Karunanidhi lost control over his family, his district leaders and other musclemen. Corruption and land grabbing by DMK members became rife, and Tamil Nadu turned its back on the old man with the yellow shawl. In 2011 and 2016, the DMK lost successively to Jayalalithaa.

At the Centre, though, the DMK played its cards neatly, choosing the winning horse in 2004 and 2009 – the UPA I and II – backing a resurgent Congress under the leadership of Sonia Gandhi. Both governments needed the DMK, which got much mileage in the form of ministerial berths.

In 2010, though, the relationship with the Congress soured over the 2G scandal. The DMK felt that the Congress had made the regional party a scapegoat in what they felt was a non-issue. An angry DMK refused to ally with either the Congress or the BJP in 2014. The result: they were out of power in the state as well as the Centre. By 2016, Karunanidhi fell ill, lost his ability to speak, and his son M.K. Stalin took charge of the party.

8

THE FAMILY MAN

It was 1968 and Transport Minister Karunanidhi had set all tongues wagging. The DMK had romped home to power under its leader C.N. Annadurai and a wounded Congress party had to have its revenge.

Meanwhile, a scandal awaited and it arrived in the form of Rajathi Ammal, who had given birth to a baby girl. When asked for the name of the father by the hospital, she told the truth – M. Karunanidhi. Congressmen found out and pounced on this information with glee. Karunanidhi was already married to Dayalu Ammal. The state assembly was the stage on which the attack took place.

'Who is Rajathi?' asked a Congress MLA dramatically at the session. A chorus began. Karunanidhi, in a quandary, was taken aside by Anna, who advised him to spill the beans. 'En magal Kanimozhiyin thaayaar,' he said upon his return, according to the state assembly records. She is the mother of my daughter Kanimozhi. There was no further scandal or shaming left to be done after his utterance.

At least not in public. But Kanimozhi – meaning honeyed language in Tamil – bore the brunt of her father's secret marriage to Rajathi Ammal.

Today, Kanimozhi, a Rajya Sabha MP of the DMK, has managed to rise out of a situation of stigma and pain to become the Delhi face of the party.

'Yes, it was not easy. A lot of people use it to hurt you. It is used as a weapon also often. But one thing it has taught me is to never stand in judgement of anybody. And I am very grateful to both my parents for that,' says Kanimozhi.

Kanimozhi was always the awkward child in the Karunanidhi family. Although close to her step-brother Alagiri, there was never any love lost between her and M.K. Stalin. As for the non-political heirs of Karunanidhi – daughter Selvi and son Tamilarasu – their relationship is, at best, an uneasy one.

Karunanidhi, even as chief minister, would spend his evenings at CIT Colony, Rajathi Ammal's and Kanimozhi's home, and his mornings at Gopalapuram, where his wife Dayalu Ammal lives. While the Gopalapuram home is an old-world-style house with open gates and doors, the CIT Colony mansion was a fortress. The father went out of his way to ensure that his daughter was protected to the best of his ability.

'He has never made me feel alienated,' says Kanimozhi. 'He has never made me feel anything that way. He has never given me any reason for him to explain anything. He has never let my mother down either. There are many politicians who make mistakes or do things. And they try to hide it under the carpet or they even hurt the person. Their children are neglected. I know children who do not have the courage to say who the father is because they may not live for another day if they did. So, if you look at all of that, my father was a very, very good man that way. I am not justifying it or saying that what he did was right or wrong. But I am grateful for what I learnt from it – never to judge. What he went through is what I am today. And I am perfectly all right with it.'

Being a politician's daughter is difficult enough. But being the daughter of M. Karunanidhi meant not having a traditional father. 'He has been a very, very busy father. It took me some time to accept that he would not come to school for a Sports Day or things like that. But then after that we found a lot in common, in books and reading and things. Maybe after my eighth or ninth standard,' she says.

It was Karunanidhi who introduced her to Periyar's writings. And his love for the written word was passed on to his daughter, a poet herself who is equally fluent in Tamil and English. Kanimozhi was also the only one amongst his children who called a spade a spade to the larger-than-life leader.

'When he was in jail, somebody gave him a set of books by a writer,' laughs Kanimozhi as she reminisces. 'I am not going to name the author. He sent that whole set to me to read. And especially because he was in jail, I felt obligated to read it. When he came out he asked me – How did you like it? I said I had read all of them but I did not like them. He was quite taken aback. He said – Why? I said I cannot agree with the way the person has portrayed women. At that he started laughing and said there you go again.'

Kanimozhi says there are several things about her father she admires and would like to emulate. 'One thing I have always admired about him – whenever there is a cherished thought or idea of his, and then someone completely shreds it apart, he gets very upset. But invariably he will come back to it and start pondering about what the other person said and whether that view was right. That is something I really admire about him. Even if he has made up his mind, I have seen him ask for opinions from everyone. It is not like he will ask only politicians, you know.

He will pick the brains of anyone he comes across. I think that is what made him grow also,' she says.

In 2007, Kanimozhi took a reluctant step into politics. 'I never wanted to be a politician because I always thought that I did not want to become part of an organization. Then, at one particular point, my father wanted me to. He did not do much explaining. He said – Now we want you to come. Of course, there are some people he knew I couldn't say no to and he sent them to convince me. So, I said yes,' she says. The family was at loggerheads and Karunanidhi perhaps did not want his favourite daughter out in the cold.

'Maybe I was one person who told him what I felt,' says Kanimozhi when asked whether her father had a soft corner for her, as the talk went. 'Of course, I respected him. That is it. I don't think he had a soft corner for me. Maybe I talk a lot to him and say things which others wouldn't because it would be disrespectful. I got away with saying a few things. It's not that you get away completely. Of course, he will give you a dressing-down and tell you exactly what he thinks.'

Kanimozhi remembers instances when she refused to toe her father's political line and spoke out instead on specific issues. 'I had written a piece on Kannagi [a woman who burnt down Madurai, according to Tamil history] – it was completely against what the Dravidian movement portrays. I respect her for the courage she had to question the king. But people like to see her as a chaste woman and I don't think we should celebrate things like that. It did create some embarrassment for him. I think when the Khushboo issue came, I spoke out against the PMK. But he did not give me a dressing-down at that time.' Actor Khushboo found herself in the midst of a violent controversy in 2005 after she gave an interview to a publication advocating safe premarital sex and was attacked by the cadre of the Pattali Makkal Katchi (PMK).

When the 2G scandal hit the DMK and its first family hard, Karunanidhi had tears for his daughter who was jailed. 'I felt very bad for him because I did not want to become part of Kalaignar TV and he even spoke about it in public. He convinced me that he wanted me to be there, so he felt really guilty and he kept saying – I forced you into this and finally this has happened. I said I am not interested, I don't believe in that whole television thing and it will be very difficult for me to digest a lot of things there. But finally he convinced me because he wanted it to be a family-run thing. But he felt very, very, very bad. And he knew actually what happened and how I would never be bothered about what happened at Kalaignar TV and I was completely clueless as to what was going on. And I think that made him feel really bad. He came regularly to jail, and every time he used to feel bad. I told him it's an experience and that I was learning a lot and I was reading a lot. I used to tell him that. He knew that I wasn't making any decisions at Kalaignar TV.'

Not many within the DMK will speak openly of the feuds within the first family of Tamil Nadu. Blood brothers at war, uncles and nephews at each other's throats and those who married into the family taking sides and egging factions on – this was the Karunanidhi family by the 2000s, when the party came back to power, albeit with a slim margin.

THE BROTHERS INCORRIGIBLE

In the 1980s, an exasperated father packed his elder son off to Madurai to oversee party affairs there. Bickering and jostling for power had begun between M.K. Alagiri and younger brother M.K. Stalin, both born to Dayalu Ammal and Karunanidhi.

Karunanidhi's eldest son, M.K. Muthu, born to his first wife Padmavathi, had long since bitten the political dust. He had been propped up as an MGR lookalike when the party splintered in the

1970s. Muthu could not live up to the expectations of him in the cine field and subsequently disappeared from Kollywood after a few films. There were reports of his joining the AIADMK subsequently but he slowly faded away into oblivion. Today, Muthu is an ailing man who lives in Chennai's suburbs in relative penury.

But Karunanidhi's second wife Dayalu Ammal's progeny did much better. Stalin's steady rise in the party since the Emergency days and Karunanidhi's indulgence had angered the elder sibling. The state, in a sense, was carved up between the brothers.

Alagiri went on to build a fiefdom of his own in Madurai and southern Tamil Nadu. He rose to notoriety with the Thirumangalam Formula – the beginning of large-scale money distribution to voters during the by-polls in Thirumangalam, near Madurai, in 2009. He was seen as favouring gangs, violence, goondaism and crime. By 2014, he was at the peak of his powers, with the reputation of a feared don in southern Tamil Nadu who would let nothing and no one stand in his way.

Stalin, on the other hand – despite the allegations, in his younger days, of womanizing, harassment of women, even abduction – cleaned up his act and his image after the Emergency jail term. Karunanidhi trained him to work and rise through the ranks. He was, by all indications, the chosen son, the one who would be his political heir. Stalin, though, would never be anointed as such by his father. It was only after the ailing old man could not speak any longer that the party leadership appointed Stalin as the working president. Karunanidhi, though ailing, remains the president of the DMK.

As Alagiri was strengthening his hold over Madurai and surrounds, Stalin was doing the same in northern Tamil Nadu. Alagiri used every opportunity to criticize and humiliate Stalin while speaking to the media. Elders of the party advised him to refrain from such acts as it would damage the party internally. But the elder son, perhaps of the view that the mantle of leadership of the party rightfully belonged to him, and slighted by its denial, refused to be controlled. He continued to spew more venom at his younger sibling. Stalin, for his part, remained largely silent – not taking the bait and refusing comment on Alagiri at media interactions.

The crisis hit a crescendo in an unexpected manner. In May 2007, the Tamil newspaper *Dinakaran*, owned by the Maran brothers – Kalanidhi and Dayanidhi – published an opinion poll on who would be the next-rung choice of leader for the DMK after Karunanidhi. The survey results showed Stalin as the clear leader, with 70 per cent of votes polled. Alagiri and Kanimozhi polled 2 per cent each.

The poll created ripples within the DMK family. Alagiri was furious. Stalin maintained a stoic silence. But the reaction from Karunanidhi was perhaps most frightening of all. 'When I am alive, how dare they conduct a survey about who will succeed me?' an angered Karunanidhi reportedly shouted at close associates.

Mayhem broke out. Alagiri's men descended on the Madurai office of *Dinakaran* and torched the building. Three people died in the fire.[1] The DMK leadership swung into action, issuing a resolution authorizing party president Karunanidhi to take necessary action to remove Dayanidhi Maran as the Union IT minister from the UPA cabinet. Maran swiftly resigned before the DMK could sack him. In Madurai, seventeen people were arrested for the *Dinakaran* attack. Two years later, all of them were acquitted.

As for the elder Maran, Kalanidhi, owner of a vast media and cable network empire in the south, he was unceremoniously thrown out of the DMK party headquarters – also the hub of news operations for the Sun Network group of television channels which had thus far been the mouthpiece for the DMK.

The space vacated by Sun TV became the office of Kalaignar TV, a new television channel begun to replace the Maran-owned channels. Dayalu Ammal and Kanimozhi were made nominal directors of the channel as Sharath Kumar Reddy took over operations.

With Alagiri in Madurai, district strongmen such as K.N. Nehru in Trichy, E.V. Velu in Tiruvannamalai, Ponmudy in Villupuram, Veerapandi Arumugam in Salem and the Maran brothers who had a stranglehold over the cable distribution network in the state with their Sumangali Cable Vision (SCV) – things had gone out of hand for Chief Minister Karunanidhi.

This was also the period when allegations of goondaism and large-scale land grabbing by DMK workers and district heavyweights surfaced. The situation got so bad by 2011 that Jayalalithaa romped home with a massive majority in the state elections in May 2011, on the back of a campaign that shredded the DMK. The party was decimated and would lick its wounds, out of power, for two consecutive terms.

Kanimozhi defended the party on these allegations. 'A lot of it was the perception which was created. A lot of people, who were completely unconnected with the DMK, were using the party's name. Another thing is that the press has always had the courage to write in criticism of the DMK. You don't get defamation cases, you don't get thrashed, you may even get a policeman to protect you. And, you know, today when he is unable to speak and is unwell, there are people who come and tell me – He gave us the freedom to write – and I think we criticized him too much. So, I think there might have been mistakes. It is not that we were above it. In some places, it did happen also. But we also needed the time to correct it. But the perception has been created – which is quite unfair,' she says.

The district leaders apart, in-fighting and open hostilities between the power-hungry siblings gave Karunanidhi a headache. As he waited and hoped that the rivalry would ease, the younger brother took action. Slowly he replaced the cadre in Alagiri's strongholds with his own loyalists, eating into the volatile Alagiri's base.

Come 2014 and the time was ripe to strike. Egged on by Stalin, Karunanidhi struck back hard, just before the country went to polls. Alagiri's key aides were kicked out of the party on Stalin's recommendation and the elder brother hollered. More and more aides were thrown out. Alagiri was meant to be provoked and he took the bait.

In late January 2014, a furious Alagiri arrived at his father's residence in Gopalapuram, Chennai. Later in the day he was suspended. Some weeks later, he was expelled from the party altogether.

'You might have listened to his interview to a news channel,' Karunanidhi told reporters after this. 'He has nurtured an inexplicable hatred for Stalin. On 24 January, he entered my bedroom ... and told me that Stalin would die in three or four months. The words are enough to break my heart.' He went on to ask reporters if any party worker would call on his leader at 6 in the morning and wake him up rudely to make a complaint about another party worker.[2]

Alagiri's fiefdom was subsequently broken up for good by Stalin. He also began playing a much larger role in party affairs – selection of candidates for polls, disciplinary actions and playing a key role in creating an election manifesto for the party.

During the 2014 elections, in fact, Stalin tendered an apology to a layperson who had met him during campaigning in Madurai to complain about the goondaism of the DMK under Alagiri. Stalin reportedly told the voter that mistakes had been made and that the DMK was committed to rectifying them. Tamil Nadu's electorate, though, did not believe his words entirely – they sent thirty-seven AIADMK MPs and two NDA candidates to the Lok Sabha in 2014. The DMK was stymied with zero MPs in Parliament.

While all has been peaceful for some time now within the first family of the DMK, the gossip and the scurrilous insinuations had taken their toll on the party and family for many years. 'I feel really bad, you know,' Kanimozhi says. 'Everyone has fights, every family has people who don't talk to each other. Your mother or your brother doesn't talk to you for a few days – you know, it's normal. You don't talk to each other for six months and then you're back and there's nothing to it. But then it happens to them and it becomes a big deal. It is very difficult. But it comes with the territory. It is like anybody in the public eye. I mean, every husband and wife have a misunderstanding and a showdown. But if it is a film star couple, then everybody is waiting there and everybody is waiting for a divorce notice to come.'

Today an uneasy peace has been brokered. Alagiri, who went silent for a couple of years after his expulsion from the party, has once again begun criticizing his younger brother for three successive election losses – in the 2014 general elections and in the 2011 and 2016 assembly polls. But his organizational back has been broken and he has been rendered irrelevant. Kanimozhi, who was closer to the elder sibling, has made her peace with Stalin, ensuring that her space within the DMK is protected. While not much love is lost between the two, they are civil in public appearances and refrain from offering negative comments about the other. The party now belongs to Stalin and his loyalists. Dissenters have either left or fallen in line, forced to complain about Stalin and his ways in secrecy.

9

HE WHO TOUCHED MANY LIVES

This final part of the book is devoted to some little-known anecdotes about Karunanidhi's interactions with his junior colleagues and his mentorship of them. For all his faults, Karunanidhi was capable of inspiring extreme loyalty amongst his party colleagues and they have remained emotionally attached to the elderly politician even after age overtook him. It also looks at what his peers across the political spectrum think of him.

SONIA GANDHI: 'TWO CENTURIES OF POLITICS'

Former Congress president Sonia Gandhi and Karunanidhi's rapport was evident from the days of UPA-I. Karunanidhi often professed respect and admiration for Gandhi. On his ninety-third birthday in 2017, as Karunanidhi lay at his home, unwell, a massive public rally was organized to commemorate the occasion. Then vice-president of the Congress, Rahul Gandhi, and other leaders from across the country arrived in Chennai to attend the function.

Sonia Gandhi, who herself was not keeping well, sent a personal letter to Karunanidhi wishing him a long life. Here is an excerpt from the *Times of India*.

> In a letter to Karunanidhi, which was released by DMK party headquarters to media, Sonia said only a few leaders' lives and works had straddled two centuries. 'Beginning in the 1940s, Karunanidhi's political life dominated the better part of the 20th century and remains an important factor in the 17 years of the 21st century. In the office or outside, Karunanidhi has been (since 1969) one of the two poles that defined the politics of Tamil Nadu,' she said.
>
> Sonia said Karunanidhi lived and breathed politics but there was much more that made him a rare and complete person. 'He was a journalist, novelist, short story writer, poet, playwright, scriptwriter, actor, producer of films and above all an acknowledged Tamil scholar. His commentaries on Thirukkural and Tolkappiam are considered important contributions to the study of the two ancient Tamil texts,' said Sonia. She acknowledged Karunanidhi's support to the Congress in 1971, 1980, 2004 and 2009.[1]

MANMOHAN SINGH: 'IMPRINT ON POLITICAL LANDSCAPE'

In 2004, on Karunanidhi's eighty-first birthday, then Prime Minister Manmohan Singh sent him wishes that were read out at a public meeting held to felicitate him. The *Hindu* records his message:

> Your political journey of over six decades has indeed largely shaped the destiny of Tamil Nadu from its nascent days. You,

drawing inspiration from the late revered C.N. Annadurai and other towering personalities of the Dravidian movement, could imbibe the best of their original thoughts and marry them with national aspirations. Your contribution to the development of Tamil language has impressed me to a great extent and this has endeared you to the millions of Tamil-speaking people all over the world ... Your political sagacity, administrative acumen and inner strength to feel the pulse of the people have left an imprint on our political landscape, and future generations of political leaders will be inspired by your example. I send you my best wishes for sustained good health and many more years of service to the nation.[2]

KAMAL HAASAN: 'HE TAUGHT ME TAMIL'

Ahead of Karunanidhi's ninety-third birthday in 2017, actor Kamal Haasan recorded and released a video message wishing the DMK leader. Here is a translation from Tamil of his message:

Kalaignar's dialogues were like a gate pass for cinema and theatre artistes. The actor who could say the lines penned by him is said to have 'arrived' in acting. Just as one proves their swimming skills by jumping into a lake and swimming, during those days, when an actor was asked – Can you act? – he would recite Kalaignar's lines in Sivaji's voice. This was an elementary study for all actors. When I was three and a half years old, I would say those lines without a change in rhythm. Everyone who heard me would feel very happy that such a small boy was able to even remember those lines. As a kid, I have recited these dialogues to both Kalaignar and to Sivaji.

I had not been close to Kalaignar ... Later, when I acted in the film *Sattam En Kaiyyil* (The law is in my hands), Kalaignar had come for the 100 days' function. That was the first time I sat close to him. After that I would give him a special preview of the good films I made. Whenever I did not show him my films, he would call me and remind me. That is how much our relationship grew ...

When MGR was the chief minister, I was speaking on stage at a function. I said in my speech that there are three teachers who taught me Tamil – Kalaignar, Sivaji and poet Kannadasan. The next day I got a call – it was from MGR. He said to me, 'You spoke of three teachers, but you did not include me in that list?' I told him, 'Your moniker itself is Vaadhiyaar [teacher].' He laughed and told me, 'What you said was correct.'[3]

NITISH KUMAR: 'A RECORD THAT WILL NOT BE BROKEN'

Bihar Chief Minister Nitish Kumar, who participated in Karunanidhi's ninety-third birthday celebrations in Chennai on 3 June 2017, spoke with great respect for the veteran politician. Here are excerpts from his speech:

> You may not be aware of the high esteem that we in Bihar hold Kalaignar in. He has had a long and old relationship with Jan Nayak Karpoori Thakur, a socialist leader in Bihar. And since then we have heard about and known about Karunanidhi-ji ...
>
> Whatever he has done in Tamil Nadu and, through Tamil Nadu, for the country will always be remembered by those who believe in social justice. Since 1957, he has continually, for sixty years, been a member of the legislative assembly of Tamil Nadu. This is a record that nobody will be able to break in the future. He has been DMK president for fifty years. This kind of an example cannot be found anywhere in the world.
>
> Dr Kalaignar is an icon of social justice. And the manner in which he brought in schemes for widow remarriage, fought against untouchability – his is a path of righteousness

that needs to be emulated and followed in India. When the National Front government was formed under V.P. Singh, the Mandal Commission recommendations were implemented. The reservations which were brought in for the OBCs or the Backward Classes, Extremely Backward Classes – there is a big contribution by Kalaignar in helping to bring about these reservations.

KANIMOZHI: 'JUSTICE FOR THE MARGINALIZED'

'There are some important things that you fight for which politics can accomplish in a day,' says Kanimozhi as she recalls how her father changed policy in one stroke for the cause of the disabled and the marginalized transgender community in Tamil Nadu. 'For instance, my team and I had been fighting for the rights of disabled people for years. We organized a rally for them. One day my father called me and asked me where I was – I said I was at home. He said there is some rally that is coming. So, I explained to him what the issues were. He asked me to bring them and come. He said he would wait for them, asked me to join him there. We had some nine or ten demands and, except one, everything was done in ten minutes!'

She also details how quickly Karunanidhi righted a centuries-old wrong, granting legal protection to transgenders in Tamil Nadu. 'Look at the transgenders issue also. They were not allowed to attend college, so my team and I had taken a few transgenders and were waiting for Mr Ponmudy, who was the higher education minister then. He was with the chief minister, so we were waiting for him. My father came down, saw me and asked me – What are you doing here? I said I am waiting to see Mr Ponmudy. He said okay and asked what for. I told him it was for college seats for transgenders. He left. Afterwards, that evening, he called me and asked for details. Subsequently, we became the first government to recognize transgenders as a separate gender. So, he was a person who could break barriers.'

Today, with the ill health of Karunanidhi and the demise of Jayalalithaa, it is not only Tamil Nadu but also its politicians who feel a severe debilitating political vacuum. 'It is suddenly like two very important leaders are not there, around the same time. It is a very shocking thing for the state. We are not used to not having him around to talk about issues. Even people who were against him. But he was there. That silence, I think, hurts a lot. But that is life and we have to find our way.'

'Sometimes when I read to him, I read *Nenjukku Needhi*, and I am so shocked. He went from Sangam to Russia to America. Especially the fact that he has written all this during the days when there was no Google.

'His sense of humour and wit are what kept him going. Even after watching the election results and, you know, after a point when you know you are losing, he will switch over from this mode to another and start cracking jokes and making everyone laugh. It was like the battle is over, we have lost the battle but the war is still on.

'He is very emotional more than pragmatic when it comes to issues. There are certain things that are close to his heart and he always stood by them,' she says.

DURAIMURUGAN: 'A FATHER AND A BROTHER'

'I was lying in hospital awaiting a bypass surgery,' says Duraimurugan. 'Thalaivar always treated me very affectionately, as if I were a child. "What Durai, you look dull, do you want to eat?" or "Ennayya, do you want some coffee?" He brought me up as a friend and a child.

'That night as I was lying down awaiting a bypass surgery the next morning, it must have been around ten in the night when he called me on the phone. "Ennayya, how are you?" he asked me. "Are you feeling afraid?" I said to him – "Tomorrow morning I have to undergo a bypass surgery. Will I be happy? Irukken ayya."

'He then said, "No. From your voice I can tell that you are afraid. I will come and stay the night there with you in your hospital room."

'Even today when I think of this incident, tears spring to my eyes. After my operation, when I opened my eyes after seven hours, he was the one I saw first. No one was allowed into the ICU but since he was chief minister, the hospital allowed him to see me.

'Another instance was when I took a powerful and senior leader in the party head-on. Even at that time, he told me, "Durai, whatever you do, you must protect your self-respect. I laud you."

'When I made a mistake, he would think his child had erred. When I did well, he would say his younger brother had made him proud. The relationship between him and me goes very deep. It cannot be told in mere words,' says Duraimurugan, tears clouding his eyes.

He recollects a conversation in Kauvery Hospital in Chennai when Karunanidhi was hospitalized – this was during the final stages of Chief Minister Jayalalithaa's hospital stay, before she breathed her last. Duraimurugan says that he, A. Raja and Ponmudy were present with the ailing leader. 'He said to me, Raja and Ponmudy, "If she recovers, then magizhchi [happy]. If the lady passes away, the party will splinter into two. One group will ask for your support to form government – they will ask you to give support for a coalition. Or they will say you give outside support. Or they will say you form government and we will give you support. You must never ally with any of them in any fashion. If you join them, you will be doomed in the future,"' recalls Duraimurugan.

A. RAJA: 'IDEOLOGY AND TOLERANCE'

'I first met Thalaivar in 1993 – when Vaiko left the DMK, there was a vacuum,' says A. Raja. 'I was a practising lawyer then. At that time, DMK needed the support of lawyers and I began to work for them. I was close to Murasoli Maran. When Maran was in hospital, I was the health minister and I had to keep in touch with our Leader to give him reports on Maran's health. That is how I got close to him.'

It was in 2002 that Raja caught Karunanidhi's eye. 'Thalaivar spoke on stage once that the meaning of Hindu is a thief. The BJP and RSS and everyone started hollering about this, they wanted an apology.

I was in Apollo [Hospital] at the time and Perasiriyar [General Secretary Anbazhagan] was there. I came down from the ICU to update them on Maran's health. A discussion was going on about the Hindu-and-thief issue. No one knew I was a DK [Dravidar Kazhagam] man or that I was groomed ideologically. They were talking about where it appeared in the Hindu texts that the word meant a thief. Immediately I named the book and the page number. Thalaivar asked me whether I have the book. I said yes, it is in Delhi. He asked me to send him the book. The next day he got it.

'From his own pocket, he paid for a half-page advertisement in the papers, stating the facts behind who had said the word Hindu meant a thief. He signed the advertisement as Mu. Karunanidhi and put it out.

'The person who had originally done the research and written the book was Kamalabhai Tripathy, a Brahmin, a Kashmiri Pandit. There are three or four meanings to the word given in the book – anything belonging to India, an uncultured brute and a dacoit. After that Thalaivar would call me by name, would take me along in his car. We began having discussions over art, history and culture,' smiles Raja.

Raja, a Dalit, emphasizes that his leader brooked no intolerance by anyone in his party on the basis of caste or religion. 'In 1997 at a General Council meeting in Melur, Thalaivar was the chief minister and the topic of discussion was the recent atrocities against Dalits in the area. He was meeting the district secretaries. He had a microphone in front of him. They said it was a personal clash and not a caste clash.

'Thalaivar immediately switched on his mike and said, "Velusamy, I am CM. I know what happened there. If you tell me that it is not a caste clash, then I will resign from the DMK and dissolve the party altogether." Everybody was shocked,' recalls Raja.

'When you get into politics and public life, you have to appeal to all people. When we said, "Ondrey Kulam, Oruvaney Deivam" (There is only one religion and one God) – that is a dilution. Dilution means a compromise without it being detrimental to the goal. There should be 30-40 per cent of compromise on ideology. Our leader would stick to ideology at least 90 per cent.

'He never liked anyone who spoke badly of women in public life. One lady came to him and said – I am in the party for many years but I am not getting a ticket. When Thalaivar called up the district secretary to ask him why, the secretary said that the woman's character was not good and that everyone spoke of her like that. He took off at him. He said to the secretary, "You will keep the women in your home and family safe. But you will speak ill of women who come into politics,"' recollects Raja.

Raja holds dear the ideological discussions he had with his leader. 'In politics, most people, when they get power, think that everyone should listen to what they say. But the thing about

Thalaivar was he was a complete democrat. He would bring together a number of people, and arguments would ensue. There was no junior or senior in those discussions. I would speak against Duraimurugan, I would speak against T.R. Baalu, they would speak against Thalaivar. Then he will take a decision based on the veracity of the arguments.

'There was a discussion once – why Marxism failed in India – this was in terms of caste and varna friction in Indian society. Duraimurugan, T.K.S. Elangovan and I were there. I drew from Ambedkar – the division of labour as expressed by Plato or Aristotle is needed for all countries and communities irrespective of race or colour. This is to maintain social equilibrium. One person has to grow cotton, another has to turn it into yarn, another has to stitch it and someone else wears it. One person cannot do everything. So, division of labour is important.

'Now, what is the difference between class and caste? Elangovan said there is not much of a distinction, they are almost the same. I said no, there is a difference. There is a difference between division of labour and division of labourers. A shoemaker, a barber are definitely needed in society. But why is it attached to birth? Why Marx failed in India and why caste still succeeds despite technological revolution is because it is attached to birth. I am a scavenger's son, I studied and I became a minister but I am not doing that work now. But still I am seen as a scavenger. Why? Because it is attached to birth. As long as it is like that, Marxism will never succeed in India. But that is where we [the Dravidian movement] succeeded. When we argued in this fashion, Thalaivar also concurred. "That is DMK. That is the Dravidian movement," he said. He then said if he had not met Periyar, he would have been a communist,' recalls Raja.

On language, there were further furious debates. 'There was another debate. Two cultures – the acceptance of it – one based on Sanskrit and another based on Tamil and Dravidian languages. Many people argued that Tamil came from Sanskrit, that there are only Indian languages. For two or three hours this discussion went on and Thalaivar listened, over a few cups of coffee.

'C.P. Ramaswami himself had spoken at a convocation address in Kanpur and I had read it. I quoted him and said there are two cultures. The problem is that the Sanskrit culture preaches caste through Vedas. Initially it was division of labour but later it was converted to division of labourers. In the Dravidian culture and literature, there is no propaganda of caste. There is a mention of caste but it was all about equality. If you spend an hour or two with him, an intellectual discussion would always follow,' he smiles fondly.

Raja was also given glimpses into the way Karunanidhi's mind worked when it came to politics and political leaders. 'Once there was a discussion about Sonia Gandhi. Thyaga Thiruvilakku [lamp of sacrifice], he had called her on stage once. Some seniors questioned him as to how he could call her that. Thalaivar said, "A woman born in a foreign country becomes widowed at the age of forty. She could have gone back to her home country. But there was a party that needed her. She could have dressed any way she wished, lived any way she wished. But she has adopted our culture, worn our clothes, worked for our country, speaks the language of secularism, lost her husband too." What is the big deal, you may ask. In the pre-Independence era, Dravidian movement supported the British rulers. The reason was in the non-Brahmin manifesto – that the British rule should continue because they were giving access to good education and basic necessities to non-Brahmins.

'Thalaivar said, "Annie Besant came from Ireland. She embraced Hinduism and taught caste-based politics and wanted to maintain untouchability as it was gifted by God. The country accepted her and called her a martyr. But when a woman born in a foreign land says I have no religion or caste, my earth is not just the one I was born on but also that of my husband's, a woman who proudly maintains that her nationality is Indian – why are those who hail Annie Besant reluctant to hail such a woman? That is the reason I call her a Thyaga Thiruvilakku." I don't see her as a Congress president. Through the eyes of the Dravidian movement I have made a comparison of Annie Besant and Sonia Gandhi,' says Raja.

He also speaks of his leader's untiring mind that worked without rest. 'Rest, for him, means to do something else, not to lie down or relax. If he is tired with chief ministerial duties, he will rest by writing in *Murasoli*. Taking rest after writing in *Murasoli* meant reading newspapers and magazines at home. So, switching to other activities is his rest. Apart from the time he sleeps, there is no such thing as rest as far as he was concerned. He used to love holding discussions while travelling in his car,' says Raja.

As chief minister, Karunanidhi was an unrelenting boss, exacting and demanding of his younger colleagues. 'When he was in power, all ministers would get terrified at 5 a.m. By 5.30 a.m., he would have finished reading all the papers and if there were any negative reports about a particular department, he would ring up the minister concerned. He has woken me up so many times at 5.30 a.m.,' says Raja. 'I would not attend the first call. I would clear my voice and make myself sound as if I had been up since 4 a.m. and reading. I would tell him that I had gone for a walk when he first called. Otherwise he will ask – What, you are still sleeping? To avoid that I would do this,' he says, laughing heartily.

'You will never see someone like him – so rigid about his routine. He would then go for a walk. Then he would write for *Murasoli* and hand it over to Shanmuganathan. After that he would go for a bath and then come down for breakfast. By then

Shanmuganathan would have typed it up. He will check the copy for errors and then head to *Murasoli* straight from there or to the Secretariat.

'By 12 noon he would reach the party office. He would watch the first half of Sun TV's news bulletin up to 1.15 p.m. and then head home to eat lunch sharp at 1.30 p.m. After that by 4.30 p.m. he would have appointments. By 6.30 p.m. he would go to Secretariat and come back to Arivalayam by 8.30 p.m. At 9 p.m. he would have his dinner. After that he would read a lot and put his thoughts down on paper.

'His hearing capacity was extraordinary. When ten people are sitting in a conference room and everyone is talking, he will pay attention to every single person. He can concentrate for three hours at a stretch. I cannot pay attention for more than thirty minutes, I always need a break after that. I have no idea how he managed to concentrate for so long,' reminisces Raja, unstoppably, as he holds forth on a leader who shaped him.

'We are all creations of external forces and internal forces that make us what we are. The situations that created Kalaignar do not exist today. Circumstances are what make a leader,' he signs off.

THANGAM THENNARASU: 'MENTOR AND GUIDE'

As mentioned in an earlier chapter, Thennarasu, in his very first stint as a minister, was handed three large tasks by Karunanidhi. The first was to revamp the state board school syllabus and introduce Samacheer Kalvi, on a par with the CBSE and other boards. The second was to oversee the building of the new Secretariat. The third was the building of the Anna Library, touted to be one of Asia's largest libraries.

'He called me one day into his ante room, leaned back on his sofa and asked me – You tell me all about the Samacheer process,' recalls Thennarasu. 'He then began to ask me very small doubts. I was astonished. He was asking me about the nuances of what I was planning to do. He asked me whether students would have to do rote learning. What kind of learning will this scheme bring? He asked me as if I were a child and I kept answering him.

'He finally told me, "Do it carefully. You have to bring in a syllabus that is inclusive." He showed me old textbooks and said, "I myself am not able to read this. How will a small child be able to read this? Go to Singapore and pick up the textbooks there and see how they have done it. The font size has to be large, first. Only then will children feel like studying. Improve the quality of the textbooks."

'He asked me over and over again what new improvements were being made. He wanted to introduce computer education. As we were talking, then Finance Secretary Gnanadesikan walked in and was stunned to see us like this. Thalaivar asked him to join the discussion. He had respect for Gnanadesikan and so he cross-checked whether I was on the right track or not with him.'

Karunanidhi, says Thennarasu, was quick to find faults and point them out but not in a superior fashion. He rarely chided younger ministers. 'Another interesting anecdote that I remember – we were in assembly and it was my turn to present the demand for grants for the school education department. A debate was going on. CM was sitting one row in front of me and going through the policy note we had prepared.

'After some time, he turned around to look at me. He asked me whether I had gone through my own policy note. I said, yes, Ayya, I have. He asked me, "Can you show where the word Samacheer is in this note?"' he remembers with a laugh.

'What a man he is! I felt as if the blood had left my body. I had missed out the word in the entire document. Somehow he caught it. Imagine how many people had looked through the policy note – Samacheer was one of the major policy decisions of the government. At least one mention should have been there.

'He was not angry but he pointed out that I had made a mistake. He was teaching me. He was alerting me that the Opposition could trip me up on this point. I told him, "I thought I will mention it in my reply." He said, "Mentioning it in the reply is another thing, but it should have been in the book." But nobody picked it up – not even the Opposition – except for him. After that I would check every single line and every single word before clearing it. That is what he taught me,' smiles Thennarasu.

The building of the ambitious and massive new Secretariat complex on Anna Salai in Chennai was another of Karunanidhi's pet projects in his last term as chief minister. This task was entrusted to Thennarasu. To date, he says he has no idea why he was chosen.

'He would come three times a day to check on the progress of the Secretariat. You just couldn't keep pace with him. He would come in the morning and say something and expect it to get done by the afternoon. We used to wonder how he could do it at his age.' Karunanidhi was in his eighties by then.

'The CM room got ready in the Secretariat. He came to see it. He then told us that whatever facilities are there in this room, the same should be available in the room of the Leader of the Opposition too. He even came to ensure that we had done it. We were quite surprised. He was very particular about this.

'Thalaivar had announced the date of opening of the new assembly in November. He had fixed in his mind that his government should use the building first. But then he was sceptical after seeing the pace of the work. He told me to handle the building work and said I should not go out of town without informing him. He said I had to finish the work for him. After this the frequency of his visits increased.

'But we missed another deadline. He was upset with us. How did he show his annoyance? His car would come daily from Walajah Road right into the new Secretariat in the morning, and at around 8.30 or so in the night it would come in again to check on the progress. For a couple of days, I saw the car go by on Walajah Road but it did not come in. The same thing happened in the evening. That is when I realized that something was wrong.

'I met Shanmuganathan and asked him why Thalaivar had not come to the new Secretariat. Shanmuganathan said to me, "Don't you understand? He is angry with you." Seeing that I was upset, Shanmuganathan softened. He told me to come during lunch time and that he would send me in to meet the chief minister when others were present. So, I went there by lunch time.

'Shanmuganathan went inside and said to him, "Ayya, Thennarasu has come." I could see him in the room through the slightly open door. He said, "Ask him to come," and by the time Shanmuganathan came out, he had disappeared into his ante room. Then he came out and asked me, "What brings you here?" I said, "Ayya, you are upset with me." He said, "No, no, I am not." I said, "You have not come by the new Secretariat for two days." He said, "I will definitely come. You people fix the date and I will surely come." I said, "No, Ayya, we will definitely finish it on the date you have fixed." Then I updated him on the developments. He said, "Okay, that is not bad."

'A day or so later his car turned into the new Secretariat. We were finally relieved – his anger had gone. He was very happy because by then we had finished the work. So, he knew how to deal with people – with me he used sarcasm and gave me a little push because he knew I would do the work if he dealt with me like that. He never shouted at me or anything. Once he gave that push, work sped up,' he says.

Thennarasu becomes emotional while recollecting one particular anecdote when the chief minister showed him how much he cared for and appreciated the hard work the young minister was putting in.

'In October-November 2010, it was a Sunday. I had gone to the new Secretariat to check on the work and I was sitting there at around 11-11.30 p.m. There was a phone call from the CM's secretary. He asked me where I was. I said I am at the assembly and asked him what happened. He told me Ayya had enquired as to where I was. After ten minutes, he called me back and asked who else was there with me. I said it is a Sunday, so I am alone. I am overseeing some work here. After another ten minutes he called me again. "Ayya is on his way there," he told me. It was around midnight then.

'I was at the back of the building when his call came. He said please come to the entrance side. I got a shock and I ran to the entrance – it was about half a kilometre away to the front entrance. As I reached the front entrance, the CM's car was near the traffic signal. I was worried as to what he would ask and I was preparing my responses. I was also telling myself that it was midnight, so I should keep my answers short as it was very late.

'His car screeched to a stop. He pulled down the window. Duraimurugan was with him. He got out of the car. I went close to him and started saying, "Ayya..." and began to brief him about the work. He stopped me midway. "Forget about all that, we can talk about the work tomorrow," he said. I was confused. "They told me you were here alone. So, I came to see you," said the chief minister and sat with me on the steps. I began to cry. Even today when I see those steps, I cannot control the tears. What a leader he is. What a great man,' he says, breaking down. 'Everyone used to tell me he is like a mother. I experienced it that day. He sat with me for about ten minutes and then left.'

Karunanidhi's wit is legendary and his eye for detail even more so. Thennarasu recounts yet another incident when Karunanidhi floored him with his comic timing.

'Just before the new Secretariat was ready, we had a pest problem. The entire building was filled with flies! We had to do something to get rid of the flies before the chief minister came to see the building. The next day an assembly session was scheduled to be held there for the first time. I was terribly nervous about the flies. I called in the PWD [Public Works Department] and the Corporation of Chennai to do something. We managed to get rid of most of them and then we kept some fly catchers too – hidden, of course.

'The chief minister came in to inspect. I was only worried about the flies and I kept looking at him to see if he would find out. He went around and then got ready to leave. I was relieved that he had not said anything about the fly problem.

'I went out to see him off. He turned to me and said, "I thought in that assembly there will only be MLAs and MLCs ... but I never realized there would be ML-EEs also [ee in Tamil is fly]." And then he left,' says Thennarasu, laughing uncontrollably.

10

TAMIL POLITICS AT A CROSSROADS

I sowed the seeds of confusion in the temple.
Not because there should be no temple.
But because a temple should not be a den of evil men.
I did strike the temple priest.
Not because he was a believer.
But to condemn the fact that his belief was mere drama…
Status chased my younger sister.
Fearful, she ran.
Wealth chased my younger sister.
She ran once again.
Faith frightened my younger sister.
She ran and ran until the edges of life…
Whose crime was it that Kalyani was left to starve?
Is it the fault of fate? Or is it the fault of those who quote fate to better themselves?
Whose crime was it that a thieving gang was allowed to loot and get rich?

> Is it the fault of poverty? Or is it the fault of crooks who exploit poverty?
> Whose crime was it that fraudulent priests in the grip of lust were allowed to roam freely?
> Is it the fault of God? Or is it the fault of those who thrive in the name of God?
>
> Courtroom scene in the film *Parasakthi* (1952)

These powerful lines were delivered by veteran actor 'Sivaji' Ganesan, the dialogues penned by Karunanidhi, in the film *Parasakthi*. What began with this culminated in a massive social justice movement that changed Tamil Nadu forever and rewrote its fate.

Parasakthi, a controversial film at the time, was the beginning of many such extraordinary masterpieces to come forth from the pen of Karunanidhi. He wove together stories of ordinary men and women, Tamil Robin Hoods and their damsels in distress like Kalyani, a beloved younger sister of Gunasekaran, played by Ganesan in the film.

A series of unfortunate circumstances drive the young, widowed Kalyani, with an infant, to immense suffering and she finally attempts to kill her child and herself. A man of status, a wealthy man and a priest all attempt to molest the desperate, impoverished woman though she manages to escape. The tragedy is laid bare in a dramatic courtroom scene in which Ganesan holds forth on how those with wealth, position and religious power attempted to molest his sister.

The plot is thick with the ideals of social justice, atheism and anti-Brahminism – the tenets of the Dravidian movement. The film, which was the debut of a starving wannabe actor 'Sivaji' Ganesan, catapulted him almost overnight into stardom. *Parasakthi* was also the template on which Tamil films were made thereafter. It marked Karunanidhi's coming of age as a powerful writer and keen Dravidian ideologue.

The journey has been a long and dramatic one for Karunanidhi. As it necessarily must. What began in film and brought cine stars to the highest democratic position in the state could never be without spicy twists and turns, intrigues, betrayals and foes, gloss, glamour and high-pitched emotional caterwauls.

A man respected deeply by friends and detractors alike, a politician with wit, vision, cunning and foresight, a leader with compassion and a sentimental, almost weak human at times – Karunanidhi is a man of many shades. His active, ticking mind refuses to give up despite age and health setbacks.

When Karunanidhi was wheeled out to the doorstep of his own home in 2017, months after he fell ill and recovered, the by-lanes of Gopalapuram erupted with whistles and shrill shrieks of 'Thalaivaaaa' and 'Doctor Kalaignar vaazhga'. When a frail, unsteady hand was lifted in something akin to a wave, the roar was even louder. Karunanidhi probably said in his mind those magical words that had roused his cadre for six decades: 'En uyirinum melaana udanpirappugaley…' (My siblings who mean more to me than life.)

Mortal he is, though, however immortal his followers and fans have tried to make him out to be. And as his mortal clock ticks, Tamil Nadu has been plunged into a dark spiral of chaos.

It has been a double whammy for the state since 2016. Two all-powerful leaders – Jayalalithaa and Karunanidhi – suddenly vanished from the political arena. Jayalalithaa passed away after two and a half months in hospital, breathing her last on 5 December 2016. Around the same time that the chief minister was hospitalized, Karunanidhi too fell ill and subsequently lost his ability to speak, as a tracheostomy tube was inserted in his throat.

The mantle of chief minister fell upon Jayalalithaa's trusted cabinet colleague O. Panneerselvam (OPS) following her death. But he did not last very long in the seat of power. The power centre in the party after Jayalalithaa – her close aide and confidante V.K. Sasikala – became impatient. The final verdict by the Supreme Court in a twenty-year-old corruption case, famously called the DA (disproportionate assets) case, was round the corner. Sasikala swiftly played her cards and elevated herself to the post of leader of the AIADMK, flouting the party constitution and ably aided by ministers and seniors alike.

The next step was to ascend to the chief minister's seat and, as her supporters began to plaster walls of the state with appeals to 'Chinnamma' (young mother, Sasikala's moniker) to become the chief minister, Panneerselvam had no choice but to step down. He fell at Sasikala's feet and acknowledged that it was he who had proposed that she take over as chief minister in a grand party meeting. Sasikala staked claim to become the CM.

A few days later, however, Panneerselvam made a sudden visit to Jayalalithaa's memorial at Chennai's Marina Beach. This was in February 2017. He meditated for forty minutes. Speaking to the waiting press, he then came out openly in revolt against Sasikala. His 'Amma's aanma' (Jayalalithaa's spirit) had told him to do so!

OPS had said aloud what many within the AIADMK felt but did not dare to even whisper to one another. A big split was expected within the party. But it was not to be. The AIADMK was in power with a comfortable majority and no minister or MLA wished to lose that power which would be their ticket to wealth for four more years. An added factor was loyalty to Sasikala, who had actively made appointments to many district posts, in the previous few years since Jayalalithaa's health had begun to deteriorate.

The DA case verdict arrived in mid-February and the convictions of Sasikala, her sister-in-law Ilavarasi and her nephew Sudhakaran were upheld. Jayalalithaa was found guilty too, but since she had passed away, the charges against her abated. Sasikala, on her way to Bengaluru jail, visited Jayalalithaa's memorial, muttered something and slammed her palm on the granite tomb – an oath that she never revealed the details of.

With a four-year jail term ahead, Sasikala installed a staunch loyalist, Edappadi K. Palanisamy (EPS), as the chief minister. Another nephew of hers, former MP T.T.V. Dhinakaran, returned to the party after a long hiatus as he and other members of the large Sasikala family had earlier fallen out of favour with Jayalalithaa.

For the second time, the party went through a tussle over whom the two-leaves symbol belonged to – the OPS faction with about ten MLAs staked claim for the symbol while the EPS-Sasikala faction did the same. The first time a similar tussle had erupted was in 1987 when MGR's wife Janaki Ramachandran and Jayalalithaa fought for control over the party.

Sniffing blood, the BJP-led Centre began to meddle in Tamil Nadu's politics. The state has been, historically, profoundly disapproving of the BJP and any chance to gain a semblance of power in the near future meant that the party would have to ally with a powerful Dravidian major. The DMK had a succession plan in place – Stalin had been announced the leader of the party and elevated to the post of working president. The ruptures within the AIADMK allowed the BJP a better opportunity for control, something that would have been unimaginable during Jayalalithaa's time. The Centre, armed with the power of fund allocations and a brute majority in the Lok Sabha, waltzed right into the melee.

First on the agenda was a fragile patch-up between the warring OPS and EPS factions. An uneasy truce was drawn up and OPS agreed to become the deputy chief minister of the state. Together they went to the Election Commission to retrieve the two-leaves symbol so that it would not fall into the hands of the Dhinakaran faction. They won, and just before the R.K. Nagar by-poll – which had in April 2017 been cancelled due to large-scale money distribution to voters – the two leaves became the symbol of the ruling party.

The R.K. Nagar by-poll, which finally took place in December 2017, caused a shockwave in more ways than one. Dhinakaran scripted history as the first independent candidate to have ever won a by-poll in Tamil Nadu. The main opposition to him turned out to be the ruling AIADMK. The DMK, which was initially expected to win or at least be the main challenger, lost its deposit. The BJP, which contested on its own, managed fewer votes than NOTA ('none of the above', an option for voters not wanting to vote for any of the contesting candidates).

In September 2017, eighteen MLAs of the ruling AIADMK were disqualified by the Speaker as they openly offered support to Dhinakaran. These MLAs have moved court over their dismissal and the verdict is likely to decide the fate of the EPS-led government, tottering on a slim majority.

A TROUBLED DMK

But it is the DMK that is struggling more than ever to regain lost ground. Although the party leadership is clear, the new leader is not his charismatic and intellectual father. Stalin has shown himself to be a capable administrator within the party as well as during his stints as Chennai mayor and deputy chief minister.

But a leader is more than just an able administrator. Tamil Nadu is used to larger-than-life personalities that the people can adore, worship, look up to and trust. Stalin is aware that he has none of these qualities. He is aloof and distant with the people he meets, preferring to lose every opportunity to genuinely connect with them and show that he cares.

Stalin is attempting to mould himself to adapt to the digital age, shedding the white shirts and veshtis and campaigning in regular shirts and pants. He even wears sneakers once in a while. He is overly cautious of press interactions, preferring his communications to be one-way – press statements, videos shot by his team which are given to the media, and making only one statement to the media before quickly walking away, refusing to take questions. Interviews granted are rare and questions are required to be given beforehand by the interviewer.

He is seen with the same set of DMK leaders who are viewed as corrupt, as land grabbers and are notorious and disliked in their district strongholds. To date, Stalin has been unable to act against them and make them fall in line. But perhaps that is a legacy problem handed down by his father who allowed district leaders to grow and become chieftains in their own right. So much so that even with grave charges against them the party could simply not afford to get rid of them.

Stalin's biggest boon is that he leads a massive party with an army at the grassroots. The men in red and black will do anything for their party and leader, as long as they are motivated. Can Stalin be that factor? It is difficult to tell. But after two election debacles under his watch, scepticism and derision of his capabilities as a leader have only increased.

What of the DMK itself? As the top leadership has taken a dynastic turn, so too has the leadership in the districts. Sons and daughters of former DMK district secretaries are favoured over meritorious candidates. For instance, in Thanjavur, T.R.B. Raja, son of former Union minister T.R. Baalu rules the roost. 'Veerapandi' A. Raja, son of late minister 'Veerapandi' Arumugam, is attempting to become the local leader in Salem, his father's stronghold. Across the state, sons and daughters are being given key positions – whether they are capable of garnering votes and being leaders or not.

THE FUTURE OF TAMIL NADU POLITICS

A fractured AIADMK, a DMK in churn, a barely relevant Congress, an even less relevant BJP, small caste-based parties that cling to tiny vote banks – this is the state of Tamil Nadu at present. A vacuum has developed, politically.

Into this vacuum have descended more ageing film stars. Superstar Rajinikanth and legendary actor Kamal Haasan have announced their intentions to plunge into politics. Kamal Haasan has already announced the name of his party and his flag – Makkal Needhi Maiam – translating to the People's Justice Centre.

Kamal Haasan appears to be attempting an Aam Aadmi Party-style coup in the southern state. At his party launch in Madurai on 21 February 2018, AAP chief and Delhi Chief Minister Arvind Kejriwal too was present. 'I am not a leader who is going to give you advice. I am a follower who is here to listen to what you have to say,' said Haasan at the public rally.

Haasan's politics, according to him, is neither Left nor Right, but absolutely centrist. His rhetoric is one of anger at the injustice of traditional politicians and political parties. He is, he says, one with the people. He speaks of corruption and says that he has crossed sixty years of age and he has no needs or wants any longer, except to give back to the people of Tamil Nadu in some fashion. He says that he has dedicated the rest of his life to Tamil Nadu and Tamilians. 'The army that we have formed to fight a righteous war is here,' he said, introducing his team across the districts. 'I am not a star any more. I am that lamp that you light at home. Light me and protect me within your homes and hearts,' he urged his audience.

Kamal Haasan speaks pure Tamil. He is a Tamilian. He is also a Brahmin. He is an avowed atheist, an admirer of Karunanidhi and the Dravidian movement. He projects himself as an intellectual, a well-read man able to understand and speak of complex ideologies.

Rajinikanth, on the other hand, is a Maharashtrian by birth and bred in Bangalore, Karnataka. Born into a poor family, he worked as a bus conductor in Bangalore, before arriving in Madras to attend film school and try his luck in cinema.

Rajinikanth is at pains to insist that he is a 'pacchai Tamilan' (a true-blue Tamilian). His Tamil is not as refined as Haasan's but he is the undisputed superstar of Tamil cinema. At an event at Raghavendra Marriage Hall in Chennai on 31 December 2017, Rajinikanth announced his political entry. His politics, he claimed, would be 'aanmiga arasiyal' (spiritual politics). The process of sifting through and appointing office bearers in each district is in full swing. His fan clubs have been converted into political units across the state.

At a function at MGR University, where he unveiled a statue of MGR, Rajinikanth, on 5 March 2018, made his maiden political speech. 'I have the confidence that I can provide a pro-poor government like MGR did,' thundered Rajinikanth, to loud applause. 'Aanmiga arasiyal means clean politics, politics devoid of caste and religion, honest politics – where every aatma is paramaatma – that is aanmiga arasiyal,' he said. 'There is a vacuum. There is a vacuum for a good leader. For leadership. I am coming to fill that void.'

Rajinikanth appears to be attempting to swing a political strategy that has been tried and tested successfully by none other than MGR. His rhetoric speaks of welfare of the poor, the 'giver' to the masses, the 'strong leader' who will lead them and protect them. His open declaration of faith in God and spirituality too is akin to MGR's, who was seen as more moderate in terms of religious beliefs than was Karunanidhi.

While the DMK under Stalin as well as the established and well-entrenched political parties will have the upper hand come elections, Rajinikanth and Kamal Haasan are fighting for the alternative vote, the young vote, the Dalit vote.

A younger actor, Vishal, already attempted to enter electoral politics during the R.K. Nagar by-poll. Unfortunately for him, his nomination papers were rejected as some of the people who signed his form as proposers stated that they had not done so. He did not contest but has vowed to enter politics in the next elections.

So, Tamil politics appears to be coming full circle yet again. While the DMK and the AIADMK do, in fact, remain the largest parties, commanding an equal share of votes – close to 40 per cent each – the alternatives remain stars from the cine field. Dhinakaran remains a dark horse, with 'sleeper cells' – silent supporters within the ruling party fold biding time to pull the rug from under the government's feet.

Tamil Nadu has entered yet another era of confusion and likely prolonged political instability. This has hit governance the hardest. Caste-related violence is on the rise. Crimes for gain and passion are increasing. The school education system is at its worst ever. Corruption – allowed to take deep root in appointments, transfers and postings of government staff from the position of drivers and security personnel to the top prestigious positions of vice-chancellors of state universities – is rife.

Political parties across the board agree in private that the introduction of freebies has led to ruin in terms of the finances of the state, which has the highest ever debt in its history – over Rs 4 lakh crore. Populism trumping prudence has meant that individual corporations of the state – such as power utility TANGEDCO and the transport corporation TNSTC – are bleeding the coffers dry. From a culture that encouraged bureaucrats to suggest and implement visionary schemes, the state has turned its bureaucracy into an ineffective machine that refuses to innovate.

Tamil Nadu is in for tough times ahead. It awaits a leader with vision who can take tough decisions and help turn the state around. There are, of course, those who are thankful that the age of strong leaders is over – the culture of the cult, they feel, has done more damage than good for the state. Perhaps, they feel, now with normal human beings at the helm, democracy will once again flourish in the state.

What is undeniable, though, is that a state which was once heralded as an example to be emulated across the country has slipped very rapidly on all indicators. Tamil Nadu needs to brave a stormy period.

But as Karunanidhi, MGR, Jayalalithaa and now Kamal Haasan have all told us – 'Naalai namadhey'. Tomorrow is ours.

NOTES

PROLOGUE

1 Express News Service, 'Ram a lie, Ramayana says he was a drunkard: Karunanidhi', *Indian Express*, 20 September 2007, http://archive.indianexpress.com/news/ram-a-lie-ramayana-says-he-was-a-drunkard-karunanidhi/219361/.

2 'Karunanidhi's remarks about Rama condemnable: Swamy', Zee News, 16 September 2007, http://zeenews.india.com/home/karunanidhis-remarks-about-rama-condemnable-swamy_395273.html.

INTRODUCTION

1 Tamil Nadu Budget Speech, 2016, http://www.tnbudget.tn.gov.in/tnweb_files/Budget%20Speech_2017-2018(Eng).pdf.

2 Press release by the Press Information Bureau of India, 22 July 2016, http://pib.nic.in/newsite/PrintRelease.aspx?relid=123563.

3 Press release by the Press Information Bureau of India, 26 February 2016, http://pib.nic.in/newsite/PrintRelease.aspx?relid=136938.

4 2011 Census of India, http://censusindia.gov.in/Tables_Published/A-Series/A-Series_links/t_00_005.aspx.

5 Ibid.

6 M. Karunanidhi, *Nenjukku Needhi*, Part I (Madras: Tamizhkani Pathippagam, 1975), p. 42.

7 Ibid, p. 44.

8 M. Karunanidhi, 'Autonomy for the States, Federalism at the Centre', *Hindu*, 15 August 2007, http://www.thehindu.com/todays-paper/tp-opinion/Autonomy-for-the-States-federalism-at-the-Centre/article14816071.ece.

9 Venkitesh Ramakrishnan, 'The Numbers Game', *Frontline*, Vol. 16, No. 9, 24 April–7 May 1999.

10 Swati Das, 'DMK Threatens to Pull Out of NDA', *Times of India*, 30 July 2003, http://timesofindia.indiatimes.com/india/DMK-threatens-to-pull-out-of-NDA/articleshow/103035.cms.

11 Sarkaria Commission of Inquiry (Appointed under Act No. 60 of 1952 to inquire into the allegations against the erstwhile Chief Minister and other Ministers of Tamil Nadu), report submitted in 1976.

12 'Top Ten Abuses of Power 2011', *Time*, 17 May 2011, http://content.time.com/time/specials/packages/article/0,28804,2071839_2071844_2071846,00.html.

1: EARLY YEARS

1 M. Karunanidhi, *Nenjukku Needhi*, Part I (Madras: Tamizhkani Pathippagam, 1975), p. 10.

2 Ibid.

3 Ibid, p. 20.

4 Ibid.

5 Ibid.

6 Ibid, pp. 21-23.

7 Ibid, pp. 26-27.

8 Ibid, p. 42.

9 Ibid, p. 44

10 Ibid, p. 45.

11 Ibid, pp. 50-51.

12 Ibid, pp. 73-74.

13 Ibid, p. 74.

14 Ibid, pp. 68-69.

15 Ibid, pp. 72-73.

16 Ibid, p. 82.

17 Ibid, p. 92.

18 Ibid, p. 94.

19 Ibid, p. 107.

20 Ibid, p. 115.

2: PERIYAR AND ANNADURAI

1 Mythili Sivaraman, *Haunted by Fire: Essays on Caste, Class, Exploitation and Emancipation* (New Delhi: LeftWord Books, 2013), pp. 98-99.

2 Ibid, p. 104.

3 M. Karunanidhi, *Nenjukku Needhi*, Part I (Madras: Tamizhkani Pathippagam, 1975), pp. 102-03.

4 Ibid, p. 117.

5 Ibid, pp. 118-19.

6 Ibid, p. 120.

7 Ibid, p. 121.

8 Ibid, p. 126.

9 Ibid, p. 128.

10 Ibid, p. 167.

11 Mythili Sivaraman, *Haunted by Fire: Essays on Caste, Class, Exploitation and Emancipation* (New Delhi: LeftWord Books, 2013), p. 121.

12 M. Karunanidhi, *Nenjukku Needhi*, Part I (Madras: Tamizhkani Pathippagam, 1975), p. 169.

13 Ibid, p. 170.

14 Ibid, pp. 177-78.

15 www.dmk.in.

3: RISE TO POWER

1 Mythili Sivaraman, 'Gentlemen Killers of Kilvenmani', *Economic and Political Weekly*, Vol. 8, No. 21 (26 May 1973): pp. 926-28.

2 Ibid.

3 Nithila Kanagasabai, 'The Din of Silence: Reconstructing the Keezhvenmani Dalit Massacre of 1968', Tata Institute of Social Sciences, *SubVersions* journal, Vol. 2, No. 1 (2014): pp. 105-30.

4 Ibid.

5 Mythili Sivaraman, 'Gentlemen Killers of Kilvenmani', *Economic and Political Weekly*, Vol. 8, No. 21 (26 May 1973): pp. 926-28.

6 Nithila Kanagasabai, 'The Din of Silence: Reconstructing the Keezhvenmani Dalit Massacre of 1968', Tata Institute of Social Sciences, *SubVersions* journal, Vol. 2, No. 1 (2014): pp. 105-30.

7 Tamil Nadu Legislative Assembly, Quadrennial Review 1967-70, published in June 1971 by the Government of Tamil Nadu, http://www.assembly.tn.gov.in/archive/4th_1967/Review%204_67-70.pdf.

8 Ibid.

9 M. Karunanidhi, *Nenjukku Needhi*, Part I (Madras: Tamizhkani Pathippagam, 1975), pp. 358-59.

10 M. Karunanidhi, *Nenjukku Needhi*, Part II (Madras: Tamizhkani Pathippagam, 1987), p. 26.

11 Ibid, pp. 26-27.

12 Ibid, p. 27.

13 Ibid, p. 37.

14 DMK records.

15 M. Thangaraj, 'Land and Caste in Tamil Nadu', *Land Reforms in India: Tamil Nadu – An Unfinished Task* (New Delhi: Sage Publications, 2003).

16 S. Viswanathan, 'Land of Inequalities', *Frontline*, Vol. 21, No. 21 (9-22 October 2004).

17 Mythili Sivaraman, *Haunted by Fire: Essays on Caste, Class, Exploitation and Emancipation* (New Delhi: LeftWord Books, 2013), p. 135.

18 Ibid, pp. 136-37.

19 Ibid, pp. 234-35.

20 Ibid, pp. 235-36.

21 Ibid, p. 276.

22 Sandhya Ravishankar, 'Emergency paradox: Common man was largely unaffected in TN', *Hindustan Times*, 25 June 2015, https://www.hindustantimes.com/comment/emergency-paradox-common-man-was-largely-unaffected-in-tn/story-KQdXGahiXvp8a6tQhuyvVM.html.

4: CHIEF MINISTER KARUNANIDHI

1 R. Kannan, *MGR: A Life* (New Delhi: Penguin Random House, 2017), p. 259.

2 Ibid, p. 207.

3 Ibid, p. 259.

4 John F. Burns, 'For Indian Politician, an Opulent Wedding Means Political Bliss', *New York Times*, 10 September 1995, http://www.nytimes.com/1995/09/10/world/for-indian-politician-an-opulent-wedding-means-political-bliss.html.

5 Tamil Nadu government figures.

6 S. Vydhianathan and R.K. Radhakrishnan, 'Behind the success story of universal PDS in Tamil Nadu', *Hindu*, 10 August 2010, http://www.thehindu.com/opinion/op-ed/Behind-the-success-story-of-universal-PDS-in-Tamil-Nadu/article16127805.ece.

7 Sowmya Dhanaraj and Smit Gade, 'Universal PDS: Efficiency and Equity Dimensions', Madras School of Economics, June 2016.

8 Daniel P. George, 'For homework, kids asked to blank "objectionable" portions', *Times of India*, 23 August 2011, http://timesofindia.indiatimes.com/city/chennai/For-homework-kids-asked-to-blank-objectionable-portions/articleshow/9706159.cms.

9 Special Correspondent, 'Rs 6.8 crore for fixing dome of new hospital in Chennai', *Hindu*, 22 January 2014, http://www.thehindu.com/news/cities/chennai/rs-68-crore-for-fixing-dome-of-new-hospital-in-chennai/article5602801.ece.

10 Samuel Paul and Kala Seetharam Sridhar, 'The Paradox of India's North-South Divide: Lessons from the States and the Regions', Public Affairs Centre, 2013.

5: FRIEND-TURNED-FOE AND SWORN ENEMY: MGR AND JAYALALITHAA

1 M. Karunanidhi, *Nenjukku Needhi*, Part I (Madras: Tamizhkani Pathippagam, 1975), p. 195.

2 A. Srivathsan, 'The Day M.R. Radha Shot MGR', the *Hindu*, 23 December 2012, http://www.thehindu.com/news/cities/chennai/the-day-mr-radha-shot-mgr/article12059018.ece.

3 M. Karunanidhi, *Nenjukku Needhi*, Part I (Madras: Tamizhkani Pathippagam, 1975), p. 376.

4 Sarkaria Commission of Inquiry Report 1, Gazetted 3 February 1976.

5 Ibid.

6 Ibid.

7 'Tamil Nadu: The debunkers', *India Today*, 15 December 1979, http://indiatoday.intoday.in/story/dmk-leader-karunanidhi-charges-m.g.-ramachandran-government-with-shipping-deal-scam/1/427545.html.

8 Ilangovan Rajasekaran, 'When MGR fell ill', *Frontline*, 28 October 2016, http://www.frontline.in/the-nation/when-mgr-fell-ill/article9201689.ece.

9 '1989 ugly episode haunts the House', the *Hindu*, 26 March 2003, http://www.thehindu.com/2003/03/26/stories/2003032605200400.htm.

10 John F. Burns, 'For Indian Politician, An Opulent Wedding Means Political Bliss', the *New York Times*, 10 September 1995, http://www.nytimes.com/1995/09/10/world/for-indian-politician-an-opulent-wedding-means-political-bliss.html.

11 Amarnath K. Menon and G.C. Shekhar, 'Booty queen', *India Today*, 30 November 1999, http://indiatoday.intoday.in/story/jayalalitha-arrest-reveals-systematic-loot-of-public-money-puts-political-future-at-risk/1/282843.html.

12 T.S. Subramanian, 'The return of Jayalalitha', *Frontline*, Vol. 18, No. 11 (26 May to 8 June 2001).

13 T.S. Subramanian, 'Tamil Nadu's Shame', Vol. 18, No. 14 (7 to 20 July 2001).

6: CASES AND CONTROVERSIES

1 The first Report of the Sarkaria Commission of Inquiry, dated 3 February 1976.

2 Reproduced from the first Report of the Sarkaria Commission of Inquiry, dated 3 February 1976.

3 The first Report of the Sarkaria Commission of Inquiry, dated 3 February 1976.

4 R. Kannan, *MGR: A Life* (New Delhi: Penguin Random House, 2017).

5 Ministry of Home Affairs Notification S.Q.No.545 (E) dated 23 August l991 (F.No.I/1.2014/17/9l-IS(D.III) (Annexure 1).

6 Interim report of the Jain Commission, August 1997, submitted to the Ministry of Home Affairs.

7 Ibid.

8 Ibid.

9 Ibid.

10 Ibid.

11 Prabhu Chawla, 'Rajiv Gandhi killing: Jain Commission report indicts DMK for colluding with LTTE', *India Today*, November 1997, https://www.indiatoday.in/magazine/cover-story/story/19971117-rajiv-gandhi-killing-jain-commission-report-indicts-dmk-for-colluding-with-ltte-832134-1997-11-17.

12 Charulatha Joshi, 'Finally All Fingers Point To A Foreign Hand', *Outlook*, 20 July 1998.

13 Suresh Nambath and M.R. Venkatesh, 'The midnight knock that boomeranged', the *Hindu*, 8 July 2001.

7: TAKING CENTRE STAGE

1 M. Karunanidhi, *Nenjukku Needhi*, Part II (Madras: Tamizhkani Padhippagam, 1987), p. 70.

2 Ibid, pp. 71-74.

3 Ibid, p. 152.

4 Ibid, p. 166.

5 Ibid, p. 171-72.

6 Ibid, pp. 272-73.

7 Ibid, pp. 278-79.

8 Ibid, p. 281.

9 Ibid, p. 288.

10 Ibid, p. 345.

11 Ibid, p. 354.

12 Ibid, p. 358.

13 Ibid, pp. 463-64.

14 M. Karunanidhi, *Nenjukku Needhi*, Part III (Chennai: Tamizhkani Padhippagam, 1997), p. 366.

15 M. Karunanidhi, *Nenjukku Needhi*, Part IV (Chennai: Tamizhkani Padhippagam, 2003), pp. 228-29.

16 Ibid, pp. 343-44.

17 Ibid, pp. 463-64.

18 M. Karunanidhi, *Nenjukku Needhi*, Part V (Chennai: Tamizhkani Padhippagam, 2013), pp. 36-37.

19 Ibid, pp. 46-47.

8: THE FAMILY MAN

1 S. Vijayakumar, '3 killed as newspaper office is set on fire', *Hindu*, 10 May 2007, http://www.thehindu.com/todays-paper/3-killed-as-newspaper-office-is-set-on-fire/article14761571.ece.

2 B. Kolappan and R.K. Radhakrishnan, 'Cruel remarks about Stalin broke my heart, says Karunanidhi', *Hindu*, 28 January 2014, http://www.thehindu.com/news/national/tamil-nadu/cruel-remarks-about-stalin-broke-my-heart-says-karunanidhi/article5626346.ece.

9: HE WHO TOUCHED MANY LIVES

1 'Sonia calls MK one of the two poles of TN politics', *Times of India*, 2 June 2017, https://timesofindia.indiatimes.com/city/chennai/sonia-calls-mk-one-of-the-two-poles-of-tn-politics/articleshow/58952020.cms.

2 'Karunanidhi a model, say leaders', *Hindu*, 4 June 2004, http://www.thehindu.com/2004/06/04/stories/2004060407410100.htm.

3 Kamal Haasan video message, 28 May 2017, https://www.youtube.com/watch?v=53sg6zYQmmg.

INDEX

ACKNOWLEDGEMENTS

A book is the work of many – tangled and woven into the author and her mind. Thanks are due first to my soft-spoken and good-humoured editor Siddhesh Inamdar, who tolerated my penchant for taking off after news developments and stories, forgetting the deadlines for this book. Working with a journalist can never be easy, and Siddhesh has done a remarkable job of letting me be and setting sharp deadlines when I went off the radar occasionally. Thank you, Siddhesh. Without your persistence, this would not have been possible. Thanks too to Deepu Sebastian Edmond, who recommended me to Siddhesh. To the unknown people at HarperCollins who worked hard on making this book better – thank you, all.

A special 'thank you' to Mr Mukund Padmanabhan, Editor-in-Chief of the *Hindu*, who immediately and without second thought consented to write the Foreword. Mr Padmanabhan is a reporter's editor, a rare breed to be respected. Needless to say, I have learnt a lot from my few interactions with him.

Researching Karunanidhi has been an uphill task. I am certain no one can do justice to a story on his life – I have barely scratched the surface. In sixty years of public life, prolific writing and speeches, and innumerable schemes introduced, Karunanidhi has been nothing short of a political legend in the country. I did not study Tamil in school and it was Karunanidhi who, indirectly, taught me the language. Between 2006 and 2011, when he was chief minister, I was a cub reporter and forced to read all of his convoluted press releases and statements in Tamil. Many seniors have helped me understand the double-edged sentences that he is famous for. For this book, thanks are due to my friend and former colleague Mr K. Parthiban, who willingly helped with translations of difficult words and context. Thanks are also due to Mr K. Ramanujam, who has pointed me in the right direction many a times in terms of the macro perspective of Tamil politics. He has worked with three chief ministers, and his vast experience has helped me gain context of a time and regime during which I was a child. Thank you also, sir, for the help with translations of phrases and words.

I must thank Mr Duraimurugan, Ms M.K. Kanimozhi, Mr N. Ram, Mr A. Raja, Mr Thangam Thennarasu, Mr Shanmuganathan, Mr Dinesh (who tried very hard to get me an appointment with Mr M.K. Stalin), Mr C. Ponnaiyan, Ms V. Geetha, Mr T.K.S. Elangovan and scores of other DMK and AIADMK leaders and workers who have, over the years, spoken with me at length and patiently helped me hone my understanding of Dravidian politics. Geetha ma'am, it all started with your book *Suyamariyadhai Samadharmam* over a decade ago. Thanks also to Mr C. Lakshmanan, Mr Stalin Rajangam, the late Mr Gnani Sankaran and the late Mr 'Cho' Ramaswamy, who have over the years spent time with me to help me understand Tamil Nadu politics. Their vastly different takes on political history have only served to enrich my knowledge.

A very special 'thank you' is due to Dr Lakshmi Vijaykumar, who pushed and shoved and guilt-tripped and cajoled me over nine months until I finished the book. This would not have been possible without you, ma'am. Thanks too to my friend Dr Kripa Jagannathan, who patiently listened as I told her tales about political leaders and had my back at every turn.

I have left the best for the last. Prem Shanker, husband, best friend, critic and champion, who was the alarm clock, reminding me constantly about the book and needling me to finish it. He is also the one who listened patiently and suggested changes as I read out every chapter. My mother, Sundari Ravishankar, my biggest fan and my sharpest critic, who was and is a source of strength and encouragement, for reading and reviewing my work, critiquing without mercy and lauding me on to do better, believing in me unblinkingly even when none else would. Father P.S. Ravishankar, who is always proud and only kept asking when the book would be out. Little brother (who is not so little any more) Sandheep Ravishankar, who is always there with words of encouragement and horrible jokes meant to cheer you up when the going gets tough, and whose love and affection I take for granted.

And, finally, thank you to my furry babies – Cheecha, Chakli, Kabali and little Kaala aka Papaya – the ones who keep me sane and grounded.

As always, there are many names left out to whom thanks are due in various contexts. To the many who have touched my life, taught, grilled, challenged, criticized but never let me hit the ground too hard – Nandri.

ABOUT THE AUTHOR

Sandhya Ravishankar is a journalist based in Chennai, Tamil Nadu. She has been working since 2005 across media and states. In 2014, she decided to go solo and began to freelance. Her investigative stories and analyses of politics have appeared in a variety of national and international publications.

She has a number of groundbreaking stories to her credit, including her extensive exposé of illegal beach sand mining in Tamil Nadu as well as that of the flawed arithmetic in J. Jayalalithaa's acquittal in the Karnataka High Court in a corruption case. She was also the first to expose the delayed decision-making on the part of the Tamil Nadu government in the release of water from the Chembarambakkam reservoir which contributed in large part to the Chennai deluge of 2015. She covers politics, social inequality, human rights, development and policy.

Sandhya has worked as a news reporter and producer for ten years with national television news platforms such as CNN News18, Times Now, CNBC-TV18 and others. She has also been part of the core launch team for news channels ET Now and Puthiya Thalaimurai (Tamil). As a freelancer, she has written for the *Guardian*, Al Jazeera Online as well as the Wire, FirstPost, the *Economic Times, Hindustan Times* and others.

When she is not working, Sandhya loves to travel and spend time with her four mongrels. She also rescues animals in distress – squirrels, donkeys, pups, pigeons, crows, ducks and the like.